Quality Management in Archaeology

edited by

Willem J. H. Willems and Monique H. van den Dries

Oxbow Books

First published in the United Kingdom in 2007. Reprinted in 2016 by
OXBOW BOOKS
10 Hythe Bridge Street, Oxford OX1 2EW

and in the United States by
OXBOW BOOKS
1950 Lawrence Road, Havertown, PA 19083

Paperback Edition: ISBN 978-1-84217-275-9
Digital Edition: ISBN 978-1-78297-570-0

A CIP record for this book is available from the British Library

For a complete list of Oxbow titles, please contact:

UNITED KINGDOM
Oxbow Books
Telephone (01865) 241249, Fax (01865) 794449
Email: oxbow@oxbowbooks.com
www.oxbowbooks.com

UNITED STATES OF AMERICA
Oxbow Books
Telephone (800) 791-9354, Fax (610) 853-9146
Email: queries@casemateacademic.com
www.casemateacademic.com/oxbow

Oxbow Books is part of the Casemate Group

Contents

List of contributors

Mircea Angelescu has worked since 1991 as an archaeologist in the Institute of Archaeology "V. Pârvan" of the Romanian Academy of Sciences. Since 1982 he has participated in archaeological excavations at the Greek and Roman site of Histria (an ancient Greek colony on the western shore of the Black Sea). Since 1999, Dr. Angelescu has also been employed by the Ministry of Culture, where he was head of the Archaeological Service (1999–2001), director of the Archaeological Directorate (2001–2003) and director of the Historical Monuments and Museums (2003–2005). In 2000 he signed the affiliation of Romania to *Europae Archaeological Consilium*. Since 2001 he has represented Romania in this and other European organisations.

Jean-Paul Demoule is the president of the *Institut National de Recherches Archéologiques Preventives* (INRAP), a public establishment in charge of most preventive (rescue) archaeological operations in France. Formerly a professor of archaeology at the University of Paris I (Pantheon-Sorbonne), he is a specialist of the European Neolithic, Bronze and Iron Ages. Since the 1970s he has been among the initiators of an innovative systematic regional programme of rescue archaeology in the Aisne valley, and he has also conducted research on the Balkan Neolithic in Bulgaria and in Greece. His research interests also include the historiography of archaeology, and notably the 'Indo-European problem'.

Monique van den Dries has been archaeology inspector of the Netherlands Inspectorate for Cultural Heritage (*Erfgoedinspectie*) since 2002. She studied prehistory at Leiden University and has a PhD (1998) on the application of artificial intelligence techniques for the analysis (and education) of use wear traces on flint artefacts. As an employee of the Council for Dutch Archaeology (*Stichting voor de Nederlandse Archeologie*), from 1995 till 1999, she was co-initiator and editor of the Dutch archaeological journal *ArcheoBRIEF*. From 2000 she was project manager at the Dutch State Archaeological Service (*Rijksdienst voor het Oudheidkundig Bodemonderzoek*). She has published on various aspects of heritage management.

Neal Ferris has worked for the Province of Ontario as a Regional Archaeologist for the past 20 years. He is responsible for archaeological programmes and issues in southwestern Ontario (west of Toronto). His own research has focussed on the lived life and identities of indigenous and non-indigenous peoples in the lower Great Lakes, and on the discourses of identity that archaeology shapes, and is shaped by, today. He recently completed his PhD at McMaster University thanks to a professional development opportunity provided by his employer. This allowed him to achieve the twin, important aims of pursuing research and avoiding moving into senior management.

Margaret Gowen is owner/manager of a commercial archaeology company in Dublin, Ireland. She has worked in commercial sector archaeology since the early 1980s and established her company in 1990. She has been active since that time in seeking the improvement of archaeological practice, research, publication and quality control in the Irish commercial sector. Currently vice-chair of IAI (Institute of Archaeologists of Ireland), and vice-president of the European Association of Archaeologists (EAA), she has been responsible in recent years for overseeing the creation of a CPD (continuing professional development programme) for IAI, which is in its pilot phase in 2006.

Peter Hinton is chief executive of the Institute of Field Archaeologists (IFA), a professional association dedicated to promotion of good practice in archaeology. An amateur archaeologist turned professional, he studied prehistory and archaeology at the University of Sheffield and held a succession of posts in London archaeology, including as Head of Specialist Services at the Museum of London Archaeology Service where he managed post-excavation work, publications and other specialist activities. He serves on numerous committees relating to heritage matters. At the IFA he works to develop quality assurance systems enabling self-regulation of archaeologists, and lobbies government and other decision makers to make use of these. Other IFA initiatives relate to the creation of a career structure for archaeologists and improvements to their terms and conditions of employment.

David Jennings has been involved in commercial archaeology for twenty years, spending most of his career at Oxford Archaeology. Now chief executive, he has formerly worked in most aspects of the organisation, but much of his career was spent dealing with post-excavation projects. As he became involved in the complexities of management, he took the opportunity to study business and has maintained an interest in the application of business principles to archaeology.

Per Lekberg has a PhD in archaeology from Uppsala University (2003), and his main research interests are the interaction, social structure and material culture of the European Bronze Age, and the history, politics and ideologies of use of archaeology in contemporary society. He is an executive officer at the National Heritage Board (*Riksantikvarieämbetet*) of Sweden, where he works on the development of strategies, regulations and guidelines for Swedish contract archaeology and heritage management.

Dáire O'Rourke worked as a contract archaeologist both in the field and in post excavation work for a number of years, after completing a Masters degree in Archaeology at University College Dublin I. She subsequently joined the Medieval Trust as researcher, and later became curator and assistant director on the Dvblinia Project, a medieval heritage centre situated beside Christ Church Cathedral, Dublin. In 1995 she was appointed as an archaeologist with Dublin City Council. In 2001, she was offered the position of senior archaeologist with the National Roads Authority where her role is to formulate a coherent and consistent approach and to develop policy and strategy in relation to the archaeological aspects of national road schemes.

Evan Peacock is an associate professor of anthropology and a senior research associate with the Cobb Institute of Archaeology, Mississippi State University (MSU). He received a BA in Anthropology from MSU and a M.Sc. and PhD in archaeology from the University of Sheffield, England. He has worked in commercial archaeology and as an archaeologist with the US Forest Service. Primarily an environmental archaeologist, his published work also includes articles on site significance, archaeological survey methods, and formation processes. He has been a Registered Professional Archaeologist since 1999, and has served twice as president of the Mississippi Association of Professional Archaeologists and once as president of the Mississippi Archaeological Association.

Janet Rafferty is a professor of anthropology in the Department of Sociology, Anthropology, and Social Work and senior research associate at the Cobb Institute of Archaeology, Mississippi State University. She earned a PhD in anthropology from the University of Washington, Seattle in 1974. Her research interests include prehistoric settlement pattern change, especially the evolution of sedentariness in the Southeastern United States. She has served as president of the Mississippi Association of Professional Archaeologists and as principal investigator on a number of cultural resource management projects in connection with highway and waterway construction in Mississippi. She is a Registered Professional Archaeologist.

Jeanne-Nora Andrikopoulou-Strack studied classical archaeology, prehistory and geology at the Universities of Munich and Bonn. She finished her PhD thesis '*Grabbauten des 1. Jahr nach Chr. im Rheingebiet*' in 1983. Between 1981 and 1985 she worked as archaeologist in private archaeological firms. In 1985 she changed over to the field unit *Außenstelle Overath* of the *Rheinisches Landesmuseum* Bonn, from 1987 until 1989 as head of the field unit. From 1989 to 1992 she was head of the planning unit in the department of monument protection of the *Rheinisches Amt für Bodendenkmalpflege* in Bonn and since 1992 has been head of the survey department. In 1991 and 1992, and again from 1996 to 2000, she was lecturer at the University of Bonn.

Willem Willems is professor of Archaeological Resource Management and of Roman Archaeology at Leiden University in the Netherlands, as well as dean of the faculty of Archaeology. He studied at the University of Amsterdam and the University of Michigan, Ann Arbor. His work in Roman archaeology includes numerous articles and several monographs. He has worked mainly in archaeological heritage management, as a provincial archaeologist, as project manager and State Archaeologist of the

Netherlands (director of the Dutch State Archaeological Service, ROB) and from 2001–2006 as inspector general for archaeology at the Netherlands Inspectorate for Cultural Heritage (*Erfgoedinspectie*). He has also published extensively on various aspects of archaeological heritage management. He participated in the Council of Europe committee that drafted the Malta Convention, served as president of the European Association of Archaeologists (EAA) and was the founding president of the Europæ Archæologiæ Consilium (EAC).

The origins and development of quality assurance in archaeology

Willem Willems and Monique van den Dries

This book is about quality. It is also about some of the primordial fears of all archaeologists. Archaeologists are more or less the same all around the world. They are usually a cheerful bunch that meets at conferences where they regularly surprise hotel managers by drinking the entire supply of beer in the bar the first night they are together. They are all motivated by a deep and genuine interest in the past: that is why they chose their field of interest against dire warnings of their family and friends who – rightly at the time – suspected they would never make a buck and be condemned to a life of poverty. Or at least, that was what it was like for the current generation in power in the discipline and those that have just retired, in general those over 45.

Their predecessors had been the generations of archaeologists from before the Second World War that had shaped the discipline in its modern form and given it a place at universities and in emerging government bureaucracies dealing with the protection of national antiquities. The training they received from them was in the pursuit of knowledge about the past and they have always been devoted to that ideal and willing to endure various sorts of discomforts, from job insecurity and long unemployment to the hardships of fieldwork in remote places, the upside being such things as having a socially interesting profession, the joy of discovery, and academic recognition. That one would do ones utmost to achieve the highest quality results has always been an unquestioned, self-evident and central premise in this context.

Nowadays, it is precisely this formerly self-evident basic assumption that has come into question, because the practice of archaeology has changed a great deal in recent years. The roots of this change date back to the 1960s when environmental concerns became important. It was soon recognised that not only natural but also cultural resources are in danger and need careful management, nowadays usually referred to as 'sustainable'. This became the basis for the birth of archaeological resource management in the modern sense, the program for which was first laid out by Lipe (1974). Archaeologists became aware that their source material was rapidly disappearing while only a tiny fraction of the information could be recorded by rescue excavation. Its survival needed a different approach that required communication with the outside world, influencing the political and socio-economic decision making process, and that would include enlisting the support of the general public. In most of the western world, existing notions of historic preservation through protection of ancient monuments (national antiquities) were gradually replaced by more dynamic concepts of managing archaeological resources in the framework of spatial planning systems that govern the processes of rapid change in the urban and rural landscapes. This happened first in the United States, it started a decade or so later in many parts of Europe and has since then spread around the world.

In the US, the 1966 National Historic Preservation Act (NHPA) and the 1969 National Environmental Policy Act (NEPA) provided the foundation for new approaches to archaeological resource management (Peacock and Rafferty, chapter 9, with further references). In Canada, developments were broadly contemporaneous with those in the US, though except for federal land there is no real federal authority over archaeological resource management in Canada: this responsibility is left to the provincial and territorial governments such as Ontario, where new legislation was enacted in 1975 (Ferris, chapter 7). In Europe the pace of development varied strongly in different countries with different traditions and legal regimes (Willems 1999), as is evidenced by various contributions in this book. At the European level a foundation was only created in 1992, with a revision of the European Convention on the Protection of the Archaeological Heritage by the Council of Europe (1992) that has meanwhile been ratified and implemented by most member countries. This was followed in 1997 by European Union legislation on environmental impact assessment (Council Directive 97/11/EC) that included archaeology (note that while CoE conventions are treaties that its 46 member states may decline to ratify, EU legislation is binding, which means that evaluation of archaeological resource potential must be implemented in the national legislation of all 25 EU member states).

In addition, since 2000 there has been the European Landscape Convention (Council of Europe 2000) to which the majority of states have signed.

The result of these new legal frameworks has been that the rescue archaeology, which in Europe had dominated fieldwork starting with the small scale excavations during the post-war reconstruction effort and culminating in unprecedented operations accompanying infrastructure development in the 1970s and 1980s, came to an end. Archaeology became part of the planning process and in a non-voluntary manner: although the territorial scope of the legal obligations varies from country to country, the impact of development on archaeological resources must be considered when these obligations apply. Starting in North America in the mid 1970s and in parts of Europe in the 1980s, this has created a vast increase in archaeological fieldwork that used to be referred to as contract archaeology and is nowadays often described by such terms as 'development-led', 'developer-funded', 'commercial', 'consulting' or 'compliance-driven' archaeology. Not all these concepts mean exactly the same as, for example, in France and other parts of Europe archaeology can be described as compliance-driven or developer-funded without being truly commercial, because it remains mostly state operated (Demoule, chapter 10). They do, however, all refer to the same phenomenon which has completely changed the context of archaeology in the western world and now also elsewhere. At a global level, there is for instance the recently (2006) adopted operational policy (OP 4.11) of the World Bank for protection and management of physical cultural resources in projects that it finances. This is not law, but it is a mandatory policy that at the global level helps to strengthen the way that cultural resources are being dealt with in development planning and implementation processes. In addition, there is international guidance for dealing with cultural resources in UNESCO's 1968 Recommendation concerning the Preservation of Cultural Property Endangered by Public or Private Works and its 2003 Hoi An Protocols for Best Conservation Practice in Asia.

Because archaeological evaluation has become one of the conditions that developers have to comply with, quality has now become a central issue and it is easy to see why this is so. There are, in fact, two related but different concepts of quality involved that come from different perspectives.

PERSPECTIVES ON QUALITY ASSURANCE

The scholarly perspective

First, there is the approach of archaeology as an academic discipline that strives to achieve the best results in acquiring knowledge about the past. This is the dominant perspective of archaeologists and, in theory at least, of the administrations and politicians that make the rules. The immediate goal for archaeologists is to achieve an academically relevant result, but the ultimate goal for both parties is to obtain meaningful knowledge about the past for the benefit of society as a whole. This is formulated in many different ways in explanatory notes or introductory articles to legislation, in mission statements of national agencies responsible for archaeological resource management (see Lekberg, chapter 11, on Sweden), in codes of ethics for archaeologists, and in much discussion in the archaeological literature. These are not just high ideals, most archaeologists actually fervently believe in them.

The next question then becomes how to achieve this goal. There appear to be two fundamentally different answers to this question. One is the classic or 'socialist' approach that if society wants something for the common good, this activity should be carried out as a public task. The other is the 'capitalist' approach where such activities are left to the market, to be provided as services by suppliers. The merits of both approaches can be discussed, as was recently done by Jean-Paul Demoule (2002a, 2002b) and Roger Thomas (2002) in the pages of 'Public Archaeology', but the choice is not up to archaeologists. It is a matter for states to decide if compliance with the rules on dealing with archaeological resources is achieved by doing the work as a public service through (semi-)governmental organizations or if this is done by providing it as a service by commercial archaeological companies. In North America the second approach prevails (Peacock and Rafferty, chapter 9, and Ferris, chapter 7) but in Europe both systems are being used in various countries, sometimes even within the same (federal) country (see Andrikopoulou-Strack, chapter 2), in a pure form as well as in varying degrees of compromise.

In the present context, it is relevant to point out that as long as archaeology was largely an academic discipline and firmly within the public domain there were of course occasional disputes over alleged failures to comply with academic standards, but the issue of quality management never arose. Looking back, this lack of concern seems hardly justified with innumerable unpublished excavations, half excavated and abandoned sites, repositories full of inadequately documented and often completely deteriorated materials, incomplete or even lacking site archives, and so on. To be sure, there *are* some valid excuses for this state of affairs as any archaeologist knows, but at the same time we all know these excuses do not justify all that went wrong.

The concern about quality only came up with the introduction of commercial archaeology. In itself this is not surprising, given the fact that it was raised by people who had chosen to turn their passion into their profession without much prospect of any serious material gain for themselves. 'Digging for Gold: Papers on Archaeology for Profit', is the telltale title of one of the early publications on the implications of the changes in the practice of archaeology in the US (Macdonald 1976). There has been widespread concern over the academic quality of development-led archaeology ever since, and for good reason. That reason is not that the innate suspicions of archaeologists about the nature of working in a commercial setting are necessarily correct. The reason, in our opinion, lies solely in the fact that commercial work depends on market principles to operate, which in archaeology they do only to a limited degree (see also Hinton and Jennings, chapter 8). Most notably, buyers do not have exclusive control over the product they purchase.

The 'archaeological market' is an artificial creation that exists because the state wants archaeological information and creates legislation that developers have to comply with in order to obtain permission for a project. The product bought from an archaeological contractor is of no inherent interest to a developer and moreover has to be delivered to, or at least shared with, the state, which is an additional motive for wanting to buy it as cheaply as possible. Thus, there is no economic impetus for quality of the archaeological product and, as Hinton and Jennings point out, the more competitive the market is, the more prices go down and the quality of the archaeological result is even more in danger.

A response to this situation would be for the state, which after all intends to secure archaeological information, to provide regulatory mechanisms to counterbalance undesirable effects of the artificial market. This is indeed what happens in many countries. Controlling access to the market is one such tool: in many countries, a permit is needed before archaeological services may be supplied. Another is supervision of the market by a government agency, which is also quite common.

Various papers in this book describe details of these and other solutions aimed at controlling either the process of the work, or the product, or both.

However, a public, government-based solution is not readily available everywhere. Notably in Anglo-Saxon countries, state interference is normally limited so the problems posed by the market have mostly been dealt with through private, not public mechanisms. This has led to the creation of professional associations, that established standards of performance on the one hand, and defined ethical principles on the other; depending on the social and legal national context in countries where this type of organisation now exists, it may have a role in defining the profession, in developing systems of quality control, it may embody aspects of a trade union and be involved with training and education. The first of these was established in the US in 1976 as SOPA, the Society of Professional Archaeologists, later (1998) succeeded by the Register of Professional Archaeologists (RPA, see Peacock and Rafferty, chapter 9). In the UK, the Institute of Field Archaeologists (IFA) started in 1979 and was formally created in 1982 (Hinton and Jennings, chapter 8).

There are similar organizations elsewhere, such as the Australian AIPA (Australian Institute of Professional Archaeologists), or outside the Anglo-Saxon world in Europe for example the Spanish *Asociación Profesional de Arqueólogos de Espagña* (APAE, Querol *et al.* 1995), the Institute of Archaeologists of Ireland (IAI, Gowan, chapter 3) and the Dutch *Nederlandse Vereniging van Archeologen* (NVvA, see Van den Dries and Willems, chapter 5) They are concerned with a code of conduct or ethics, standards of performance, a register and a grievance procedure tailored to the needs in each national context. In many other countries, however, these have not even begun to be created yet. Despite the fact that – as follows from the above discussion – the need for such an organisation may not be felt in some systems (*cf.* Demoule, chapter 10) – it seems likely that this will happen in future years, as more countries change to market systems for archaeology (as is, for example, described for Romania by Angelescu, chapter 6 and for Ireland by Gowen and O'Rourke, chapters 3 and 4). Probably even more significant in this respect is the trend for international organisations such as the European Union, the World Bank or the International Finance Corporation to issue mandatory policies on dealing with cultural heritage in projects that they finance. It seems inevitable that this shall lead to a need for basic standards regarding organisations, staff, and products.

The quality management perspective

So far, only the need for mechanisms of quality assurance as perceived by archaeologists and out of academic concerns has been discussed. There is, however, another perspective on quality assurance or quality control that has been developed in engineering and manufacturing (Garvin 1988, Juran 1995, Juran and Godfrey 1999). In modern definitions there is often a difference between quality control (a set of procedures intended to ensure that a service adheres to a defined set of quality criteria or meets the requirements of the client) and quality assurance (a set of procedures intended to ensure that a service in process, before work is complete, meets specified requirements). Quality management is probably a suitable overarching concept.

It is now a field by itself, concerned with systems that are intended to ensure that products or services are designed and produced to meet all customer requirements and expectations. Hinton and Jennings (chapter 8) also give several definitions of the concept. Probably the best known and most widely used definition of quality is that of the International Organisation for Standardisation (ISO) that reads: 'the totality of features and characteristics of a product or service that bear on its ability to satisfy stated or implied needs'. However, in the present context it is useful to briefly examine the genesis of quality management.

Though the use of some aspects of quality management has been traced back into antiquity (Juran 1995), the roots of modern quality management lie in the Industrial Revolution, when mechanisation and specialisation first led to the idea of standardisation that is often attributed to the French artillery general Jean-Baptiste Vaquette de Gribeauval. He became inspector of artillery in 1776, after which he carried out reforms such as standardising the calibres used by the army (that subsequently were instrumental in the military successes of Napoleon).

Standardisation requires specification of the end product and this in turn created the need to ensure that such products met the given specifications. A logical solution is quality inspection, which was broadly used in industrial production by the late 19th century, especially in the US. This is in fact the beginning of quality management that was soon to be followed by ideas on how to control the quality of the product by controlling the process of manufacturing that were first developed by the American engineer G. S. Radford in his 1922 book on 'The Control of Quality in Manufacturing'. As Garvin (1988, 5) points out, this was 'the first time quality was viewed as a distinct management responsibility and as an independent function'.

The production levels needed during the Second World War led to further developments such as the use of statistical indicators for monitoring and defining so-called 'acceptable quality levels', and in 1947 the ISO was created. The fact that in Japan, after the war, it was senior management rather than technical staff that first picked up on quality management ideas from quality gurus such as Juran, is considered to be one of the circumstances that led to the Japanese economic boom of the 70s and 80s. Their leadership philosophy included motivation of staff as an important element, which led to a Japanese concept of the issue of how to manage quality that was termed '*kaizen*' by its foremost proponent, Masaaki Imai (1986). *Kaizen* means ongoing improvement involving everybody, step by step and without spending much money. The concept is based on an approach that is different from the original 'hardcore' American approach aimed at increasing productivity and maximising profit. In the *kaizen* concept, quality does in fact become a goal by itself and is no longer just a means to an end. It is based on the belief in an internal drive for quality that is oriented to the long haul instead of short-term results that often drive corporate goals and executive management behaviour in the west (from comments by Masaaki Imai in an interview in *Quality Digest* 17 (6), see http://www.qualitydigest.com/june97/html/imai.html (accessed 1.5.2006).

KAIZEN IN ARCHAEOLOGY?

It is clear from the above, that developments in quality management have come very close to what has been described above as the scholarly perspective in archaeology that has always aimed for quality in the pursuit of knowledge as a goal by itself. Nevertheless, it should be realised that this is the latest development in a school of thought that presupposes an organised approach to ensuring quality. It is often pointed out that archaeological work when viewed as research has to comply with the general rules of academic research that by definition require an organised approach and moreover, as pointed out by Demoule in chapter 10, 'the scientific objectives of an excavation are on each occasion local and context-specific'. This is most certainly true, as it is also true that much of the product, the result of the excavation, is determined by such factors as the dedication, skill and scholarly capabilities of the archaeologist involved.

But apart from being research, all archaeological fieldwork is also a production process the quality of which can, in principle, be improved by controlling the process of the work, the methodology and techniques that are used, the staff employed, and the end-product. This can be done in various ways, as is evidenced by the variety of approaches described in this book. Probably the most far reaching approaches to quality management of archaeological work are the standards and guidelines developed in the UK and in the Netherlands (see Hinton and Jennings, chapter 8; Van den Dries and Willems, chapter 5; Willems and Brandt 2004). Such detailed standards are tailored to the needs of the system at the national level, as is evidenced by the differences between them resulting from the way that archaeological resource management is organised but also, for example, from the differences in excavation techniques between Britain and continental Europe.

In any case it is clear from discussions provided by Ferris (chapter 7) and by Peacock and Rafferty (chapter 9) that in a commercialised archaeological market the relevance of work can be seriously compromised if a sufficient level of quality assurance is lacking even though the examples from the UK and the Netherlands make clear that all is not well when it is in place. For Ireland, with a well developed though less specific system of control, similar conclusions can be drawn (Gowen, chapter 3, and O'Rourke, chapter 4). One interesting question is whether the development of standards and guidance in countries without commercial archaeology would not contribute significantly to improve the quality and relevance of the results, even when defined solely by academic standards. Andrikopoulou-Strack (chapter 2) considers this to be the case in Germany. The Federal Republic of Germany, with its differentiated systems in the various states, would indeed seem to be an ideal testing ground to answer such a question. Given the experience in our own country as outlined in chapter 5, we believe the answer will certainly be positive, given the strongly increased performance of archaeology as a process, but also in its research output and in its social role, a perspective that has so far not been discussed.

There are thus other aspects to quality management in archaeology that need to be briefly addressed here because 'quality' cannot be simply equated to academic relevance or to the level to which legally imposed needs are satisfied.

First, an encompassing archaeological quality management in our opinion is the result of quality assurance in combination with knowledge management. A simple definition of knowledge is that it is information of which one is aware, and knowledge management implies the notion of strategies to increase knowledge by capturing information and expertise and, above all, by conscious and critical reflection on aims, choices and research objectives in a broad perspective. Another aspect of knowledge management is the transfer of knowledge and in our field this should not be understood solely as the transfer of knowledge within the discipline. It must also encompass the transfer of knowledge to society.

As is stated most clearly in Lekberg's contribution to this book (chapter 11) where he explains the Swedish perspective, and is increasingly voiced in recent discussions on public archaeology, what is at stake here is the wider social relevance of archaeology. Following the ISO definition cited above, what is relevant is the ability to satisfy stated or implied needs and the final reason for the existence of archaeological resource management is that societies have a need for it. What precisely this need is, is discussed in a wealth of recent literature (such as Aplin 2002, Carman 2002, Fowler 1992, Howard 2003, MacManamon and Hatton 2000, Skeates 2000). It is also hotly debated in the pages of such journals as 'Public Archaeology' and at meetings of organisations like the World Archaeological Congress or the European Association of Archaeologists.

This is obviously not the place to go into this discussion. From the simple fact that the management of archaeological resources is being supported by legislation as well as budgets, it can be deduced that apparently there is a contribution to the wellbeing of society. From the fact that the level of this support almost everywhere is far below even the most modest expectations, it can be assumed that in general this contribution does not satisfy the needs of society well enough, and such an opinion is certainly shared widely in the global world of archaeologists. In fact, almost all contributions in the book in one way or another voice the same viewpoint and it is evident that heritage managers see the need to add another layer to the quality of their work, one that aims for social relevance.

The concept of *kaizen* would seem to be applicable here, with step by step development both internally, in the actual work of dealing with heritage resources, and externally, in developing the tools to deal better with social needs and to aim for high quality, sustainable results in the long run. Fortunately, this is something that in our opinion fits rather well with the profile of the vast majority of archaeologists all over the world.

HOW THIS BOOK CAME ABOUT

In recent years, publications on the theory and practice of archaeological resource management have been produced at an increasing rate. However, while quality issues are one of the central concerns in the discipline, these are only – and not very often – discussed in the small number of journals dealing with management issues (see Cleere 2004 for an overview). Preparing a comparative international overview thus seemed to be a useful contribution to a field where, compared to archaeological research, international debate has only begun relatively recently.

Before the 1970s, archaeological heritage management was largely defined as monuments protection, was governed by legal frameworks at the national level and was administered by civil servants. This context did apparently not stimulate international discussion and comparison, although there was some work done on developing international standards (UNESCO 1968). Henry Cleere's 1984 book on 'Approaches to the Archaeological Heritage' was the first – and for quite some time the only – attempt to give an overview of relevant systems across the globe.

When things started to change in the 70s and 80s, the new approach to heritage resources inevitably led to more international discussion about fundamental issues. It is surely no coincidence that important new international forums came into being in this period, such as the World Archaeological Congress and the ICOMOS International Committee for Archaeological Heritage Management (ICAHM). But solutions to change existing legal, administrative and other structures by necessity had to remain national. International treaties and charters can establish principles, but they depend on states to implement those in a manner that they choose. A good example is the introduction of commercial archaeology in some European countries or states, and its rejection in others.

Where it was introduced, it has had a very strong influence on the discipline as a whole, and sometimes has led to a big gap between those in heritage resource management and those at the university. Especially in the Anglo-Saxon world this has created absurdities such as the occasional use of the concept of 'professional archaeologist' – not as a designation for someone having been trained and being employed as an archaeologist (as opposed to, for example, an amateur archaeologist) but as opposed to an 'academic archaeologist'. In continental Europe, commercialisation has generally been less and where it did occur it seems that stronger ties have been maintained between professionals in academia, museums, civil service and private enterprise. However, everywhere the profession has become segmented to a higher or lesser degree so there are different viewpoints being voiced in national debates (see, for example Reeners 2006 on Ireland); and internationally, especially in Europe with its many different systems of heritage management, different administrative systems and different approaches to ensuring the quality of archaeological work, there has inevitably been discussion on the relative merits of these. Such discussion is not limited to professional circles, by the way. A recent example is Belgium, where the political discussion about the future structure of archaeological heritage management

IS ARCHAEOLOGICAL WORK CONSIDERED TO BE A SERVICE?

YES	NO		
Germany (partial) Ireland Netherlands Romania Sweden (in future)	France Germany (partial) Sweden	YES	DOES THE STATE WANT TO CONTROL THE QUALITY OF ARCHAEOLOGICAL WORK?
Canada United States United Kingdom		NO	

Figure 1.1 The differences in the principles that govern the organisation of archaeological resource management in the countries that are looked at in this book.

in Flanders in 2005 has incorporated an evaluation of the systems in France and in the Netherlands.

The roots of this book go back to the annual round tables as well as sessions on heritage management at meetings of the European Association of Archaeologists (EAA). These have a tradition of over 10 years now, and for most of that time they have also been participated in by American colleagues and occasionally from other parts of the world. In September 2005 the editors organised a session on 'Quality assurance in archaeology' at the EAA Annual Meeting in Cork, Ireland, which generated much interest. Most of the papers delivered at that session have been included in this book, which has been expanded by other papers, including some that were delivered at a comparable session organised in November 2005 by the Europae Archaeologiae Consilium (EAC) in Rosas, Spain. EAC is the organisation for the heads of national organisations with legal responsibility for heritage management in Europe (see Willems 2000), that acts as a forum for debate, cooperation and exchange of information.

We have used the differences in the principles that govern the organisation of archaeological resource management in various countries as a way to organise the articles in this book. In our view, there are two basic questions that both relate to the role of the state:

1. Does the state consider archaeological work to be a service, or does it not?
2. Does the state wish to control the quality of archaeological work or does it not?

If these are put into a matrix (figure 1.1), this results in four different options of which one is only theoretical: we do not know of any situation where a country does *not* consider archaeological work to be a service and at the same time is *not* interested in exercising control over the work that is being done, by whatever means.

We hope this book will be of interest to a wide variety of readers, professionals as well as students, and in particular that it may provide inspiration for opinion leaders and those colleagues that are involved in policy decisions. The wide variety of approaches discussed by our contributors illustrates above all that there are multiple solutions to the same challenges, each with their own advantages and disadvantages from which we all can learn. We are very grateful to our contributors for finding time in their quite demanding jobs to produce copy and to Oxbow Books for their assistance in getting this book to print.

References

Aplin, G. (2002) *Heritage: identification, conservation, and management*. Oxford.

Carman, J. (2002) *Archaeology and heritage: an introduction*. London.

Cleere, H. (1984) *Approaches to the Archaeological Heritage*. Cambridge.

Cleere, H. (2004) A gap in the bookshelves; where are the management journals? *European Journal of Archaeology* 7 (3), 317–321.

Council of Europe (1992) *European Convention on the Protection of the Archaeological Heritage (Revised) and Explanatory Report*. (European Treaty Series 143). Strasbourg.

Council of Europe (2000) *European Landscape Convention and Explanatory Report*. (European Treaty Series 176). Strasbourg.

Demoule, J.-P. (2002a) Rescue Archaeology. The French way. *Public Archaeology* 2, 170–177.

Demoule, J.-P. (2002b) Reply to Roger Thomas. *Public Archaeology* 2, 239–240.

Fowler, P. J. (1992) *The Past in Contemporary Society: Then, Now*. London.

Garvin, D. A. (1988) *Quality management*. New York.

Howard, P. (2003) *Heritage: Management, Interpretation, Identity*. London.

Imai, M. (1986) *Kaizen: The Key to Japan's Competitive Success*. New York.

Juran, J. M. (1995) *A history of managing for quality*. Milwaukee.

Juran, J. M. and A. B. Godfrey (eds) (1999) *Juran's Quality Handbook* (5th Edition). New York.

Lipe, W. D. (1974) A conservation model for American archaeology. *The Kiva* 39 (12), 213–243.

Macdonald, W. K. (ed.) (1976) *Digging for gold: papers on archaeology for profit*. (Museum of Anthropology, Technical Reports 5). Ann Arbor.

MacManamon, F. P. and A. Hatton (eds) (2000) *Cultural resource management in contemporary society: perspectives on managing and presenting the past*. (One World Archaeology 33). London.

Querol, A., M. I. Martínez-Navarrete, F. Hernández, L. Cerdeño and V. Antona (1995) The Value of Archaeological Heritage: an Analysis by the Professional Association of Spanish Archaeologists (APAE). *Journal of European Archaeology* 3 (1), 233–246.

Reeners, R. (2006) *Archaeology 2020. Repositioning Irish Archaeology in the Knowledge Society. A realistically achievable perspective*. Dublin.

Skeates, R. (2000) *Debating the Archaeological Heritage*. London.

Thomas, R. (2002) Comment. Rescue Archaeology. The French way. By Jean-Paul Demoule. *Public Archaeology* 2, 236–238.

UNESCO (1968) *Recommendation concerning the Preservation of Cultural Property Endangered by Public or Private Works.* Paris.

UNESCO (2003) *Hoi An Protocols for Best Conservation Practice in Asia. Professional guidelines for assuring and preserving the authenticity of heritage sites in the context of the cultures of Asia.* Bangkok.

Willems, W. J. H. (1999) *The Future of European Archaeology.* (Oxbow Lecture 3). Oxford.

Willems, W. J. H. (2000) *Challenges for European Archaeology.* Zoetermeer.

Willems, W. J. H. and R. W. Brandt (2004) *Dutch Archaeology Quality Standard.* (RIA-report). Den Haag.

CHAPTER 2

Archaeology and heritage management in Germany

Jeanne-Nora Andrikopoulou-Strack

INTRODUCTION

Archaeological heritage management in Germany today is still dominated by work carried out by state archaeological services with long traditions in research and fieldwork. Nineteen state offices are in charge of the implementation of sixteen state laws all focussing on the same aim: monument protection and care. A crucial task for all state offices is to give advice when developments threaten the archaeological resource, aiming to preserve it or formulate the proper strategy for further investigation. Archaeological field work such as survey or excavation – in some federal States also involving private enterprises – is just a small part within the field of tasks to be covered within heritage resource management. Archaeology in Germany is characterised by wide variety of approaches but at the same time also a high compliance with the objective targets set by state laws. A long tradition in practicing archaeology and the precise task description in law are the main reason why German archaeology seems to make common standards dispensable. Nevertheless, there are aspects of German archaeological heritage management worth being better coordinated and improved.

REVIEW

An account of archaeology and heritage management in Germany requires consideration of the political structure. A high level of political autonomy of the individual states is characteristic of the political system in Germany since the formation of the first German state in the 19th century. The Federal Republic of Germany is a federation consisting of 16 autonomous states (the *Länder*). According to its constitution, the states are responsible for all areas of legislation not exclusively covered by the federal government. Education as well as monument conservation and preservation of archaeological monuments and historic buildings are also the legislative responsibility of the federal states (Horn 2003).

Protection of cultural heritage in Germany has a long tradition. In the early 19th century numerous archaeological societies were established, often as a reaction to the threats caused to monuments and landscape through industrial exploitation. Their aim was to protect and explore archaeological sites and historical monuments.

In the course of the 19th century some of these private bodies became provincial or national state institutions after the establishment of the German Imperial State. Many famous research projects, such as the investigations in Haithabu or of the sites along the Roman Limes, were initiated in these early years of heritage management.

Until the late 1970s management of archaeological matters was regulated by the Prussian excavation law (*Preussisches Ausgrabungsgesetz*) enacted in 1914. This law mainly focussed on excavation and finds. The law introduced state conservators, the so-called *Staatliche Vertrauensmänner für Kulturgeschichtliche Bodenaltertümer*, mostly the directors of provincial or local museums – that were responsible for the technical and scientific results.

LEGAL INSTRUMENTS FOR MONUMENT PROTECTION AND CARE

Today all German federal states have the protection of historic and cultural monuments established as a public concern in their constitution. Nevertheless it took almost 30 years after the foundation of the Federal Republic of Germany before all German states developed their own laws for monument protection (Gumprecht 2003; Martin, Viebrock and Kleeberg 2005). After the reunification of East and West Germany, five new federal states have been created which also enacted their own laws for monument protection.

Monument protection and care is a task which falls to the authorities responsible for historic preservation in every state. Depending on the law there are states with two or with three administrative levels of responsibility (*Denkmalschutzbehörden* or *Denkmalbehörden*). The supreme authority in every state is the governmental department in charge of monument protection. Upper monument authorities correspond as a general rule to districts or counties. Not all laws have established them; therefore there are federal states where upper monument authorities are missing. Lower monument authorities are in the majority towns, municipalities (sometimes also districts or counties when there are no upper monument authorities).

The most important differences between the laws are largely juridical ones concerning the procedure for protecting monuments and the legal status of archaeological offices. In matters of monument protection, some of the laws declare monuments already as protected from the moment they are discovered and scheduled, others require a formal protecting procedure that involves many different partners and sometimes also politicians. As for the legal status of archaeological state offices, some laws define them as agencies of the state, while others consider them to be only research institutions that need to be involved in the decision making process. These differences have momentous consequences for the implementation of monument protection. With regard to the tasks and the objectives, state laws are comparable to another, all of them focussing on monument protection and care.

Monument care in Germany is incumbent on 19 monument offices in the federal states. This number results from the fact that there are two monument offices in the state of North Rhine-Westphalia and that towns with a long independent archaeological tradition, such as Cologne and Lübeck, have an additional office. Furthermore, many towns have their own archaeologist who is in charge of local excavations and also sometimes performs the task of a lower monument authority.

All state monument offices are charged with the management and protection of cultural resources. They give scientific advice and furnish opinion on all matters of historic preservation. Furthermore they carry out scientific work on methods and practice of monument care, scientific research and investigation of monuments, rescue excavation and publication. All these activities do not differ from those practised since the early beginnings of archaeology in Germany and they belong more or less to the archaeological practice taught at universities.

The new laws introduced tasks archaeologists had not been trained for: state offices were enacted by law as 'agencies of public concern' and they are expected to comment on every planning application and other municipal, county or state actions in order to achieve an adequate management decision and if possible preservation *in situ* of the sites and monuments that may be affected. Only step by step the staff of these state offices became trained in these matters.

CHANGES IN GERMAN HERITAGE MANAGEMENT

The new laws led to considerable changes in the focus of the tasks of the monument offices. Developing strategies for the recording, preservation and management of archaeological heritage became a central concern. Giving scientific advice and providing advice on matters of archaeological heritage as member of an 'agency of public concern' requires broad knowledge of the archaeological resource within a given area. Consequently, major efforts have been made in the last decades in enhancing data collection and increasing the use of non-intrusive methods such as survey and prospection. Databases, often combined with a geographical information system, have meanwhile been built up in all states. Information about archaeological sites will soon be accessible not only to archaeologists but also to planners and other bodies. Within a period of only thirty years German archaeology moved from a predominantly research orientated field of study to a partner acting within the process of environmental management and development.

Research and investigation of monuments and rescue excavations

All monument offices look back on a long tradition in theoretical and practical research going back to a number of research projects started in the 19th or early 20th centuries. Usually these projects are undertaken within one German state and focus on a selected site or a group of sites. Institutions such as the *Römisch-Germanische Kommission* (RGK) and the *Deutsche Forschungsgemeinschaft* (DFG,

German Science Foundation) bring together various archaeological institutions including archaeological services and universities from across state borders and from abroad. These projects are almost pure scientific research projects comprising both theoretical and applied research, such as fieldwork.

In addition, all state services undertake fieldwork on threatened sites, mostly carried out by their own field unit. In practice, every institution has its own standards for the archaeological field work which evolve and adapt to technical innovations.

DEVELOPER-FUNDED ARCHAEOLOGY AND QUALITY ASSURANCE FOR ARCHAEOLOGICAL FIELD WORK

In the early 1990s, some of the regional monument offices, such as those in North-Rhine-Westphalia, Lower Saxony and Bavaria started to demand that the developers pay for the archaeological investigations caused by their building projects (figure 2.1) (see Oebbecke 1997 and various articles concerning commercial archaeology in Germany published in '*Kommerzielle Archäologie*' 1998). Something like the 'polluter pays' for the damage he causes. Some of the federal states – especially those founded after the reunification – have even incorporated the principles of developer-funded archaeology in their laws. In the other federal states, developer funds are obtained by requiring field work as a condition to a planning permission, *e.g.* a building permit. This approach made new financial resources available to archaeology and at the same time it opened up the archaeological 'scene' to commercial contractors long before the Valletta Convention came into effect.

The introduction of commercial archaeology led for the first time in Germany to a need for generally accepted standards. As a result some monument offices formulated written standards for field work valid in the area for which they were responsible. Alongside these, the German State Archaeologists Committee edited some written standards valid for all federal states (first published 1999 in '*Archäologisches Nachrichtenblatt* 4', *Heft* 1,12–45, revised in 2006. Available on the internet at www.landesarchaeologen.de/publ/grabungsstandards_april_06.pdf). This guidance predominantly regulates technical requirements concerning the execution of field work and post-excavation processing and is based on long experience.

After almost 15 years of developer-funded archaeology in Germany, the system is far from stable. Some of the monument offices do not accept contractors for field work, because they fear a poor quality of archaeological investigation. Some archaeological contractors in Germany work in all federal states where they are accepted, others more locally. Up to now there is a lack of generally valid, fixed criteria defining minimum scientific and technical qualification requirements for private archaeological enterprises and for the authorisation or refusal of an archaeologist. The minimum technical and scientific quality expected from a firm is still not determined.

On the other hand the contractors have, so far, not succeeded in organizing themselves into their own association with self regulating guidance. In modern

Figure 2.1 Excavations of the Rheinisches Amt für Bodendenkmalpflege in the brown coal mining area near Jülich (Photo Rheinisches Amt für Bodendenkmalpflege).

terms a 'corporate identity' is missing. The number of contracts is dependent on how much fieldwork the state office imposes on developers. Although there is legal regulation and a requirement for developer funded archaeology, the amount of archaeological investigation depends on the assertiveness of the monument office. For them, imposing archaeological investigations on developers is often a struggle. Developers still do not easily accept paying for archaeological work, since archaeological remains are often not seen as being of high value or importance. Once they have accepted that they must finance archaeological fieldwork, developers often

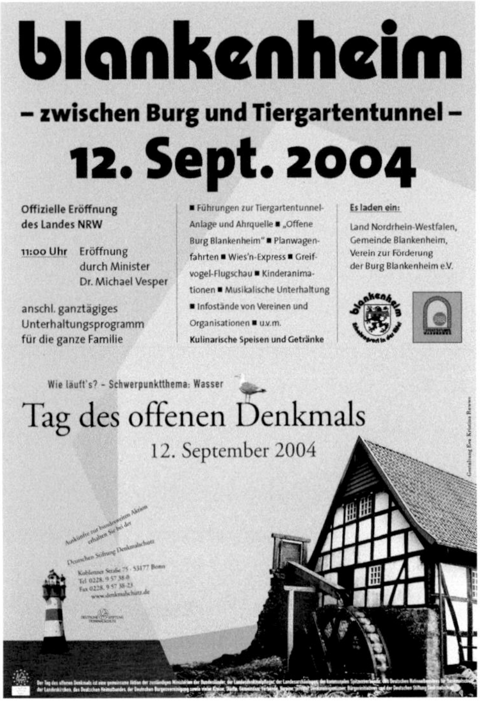

Figure 2.2 Poster advertising the 'Day of the open monument 2004' in Blankenheim (Photo Pressestelle Gemeinde Blankenheim).

try to complete the work at the lowest price. As a result, contract archaeology in Germany is carried out today at the level of the European minimum wage. This sometimes has immediate negative effects on the quality of the work.

Since there are no profile specifications for an archaeological contractor and no high level standards for an authorisation, almost any experienced archaeologist can set up a company. This situation is linked to the fact that in Germany a diploma in archaeology implies that the person is qualified to work on all archaeological subjects. Excluding an archaeologist, for example from field work, would mean banning him from his profession and this is forbidden by law in Germany. Even so, valid written standards specify some skills and experience the archaeologist must have in order to carry out work. One can only be refused after some failed work. The system is therefore based on excavation permits and the regular supervision and control of contractors' work.

The monument offices control to varying degrees compliance with their own state guidelines or – where these are lacking – with those published by the German State Archaeologists Committee. Some offices control the field work while others just check the results. Up to now there has been no systematic 'embedding' of contractors in the research agendas of the monuments offices. Their integration in the monument's office scientific targets could lead to an increase in the quality of their work and less need for technical control. In relation to the Valletta Convention, it is likely that contractors will play an important role in the future, since public budgets probably will not increase. Stressing the research targets which have to be met in a federal state, could give contractors a feeling of the important role they could play.

Bringing the public into contact with its own archaeological heritage

Informing the public about the results of archaeological work is an important task concordantly formulated in all state laws. Therefore all state services publish the

Figure 2.3 Archaeologist presenting a mediaeval fount in Blankenheim to the public (Photo Erich Schell, Pressestelle Gemeinde Blankenheim).

results of their work both as research and popular reports. This way of acting is part of the strategy followed by all state services giving the public an understanding of archaeology, monument protection and care. Strong efforts are made to open archaeological monuments to the public. As in many other European countries there is a fixed day for the presentation of cultural heritage (heritage day) (figure 2.2) and more state offices give information on current research and ongoing archaeological excavations (figure 2.3). All these actions are of great importance in Germany, where relationships to history are ambivalent.

German State Archaeologists Committee

Of crucial importance for German archaeology is the role played by the German State Archaeologists Committee, founded in 1949. It consists of the heads of the archaeological monument offices or archaeological departments within the heritage offices of the federal states. This institution performs the task of harmonising and if possible also equalising aims and approaches of the state monument offices. The involvement of archaeological services in planning and environmental processes demands the coordination of state archaeological work in order to provide coherent solutions to monument preservation and management in the context of the superordinated federal German or European legislation such as the Environmental Impact Assessment directive (EIA) and the Water Framework Directive (WFD). The German State Archaeologists Committee takes a decisive role in the process of harmonisation in German archaeology and fills the gap created by the pluralism of the German system. Therefore they hold annual congresses mostly focussing on strategic objectives and actual problems aiming at agreeing upon a common way of acting. In addition the German State Archaeologists Committee sets up working groups assigned to work out solutions for specific scientific or strategic subjects.

CONCLUSIONS

Judged from abroad, German archaeology would seem to have deficiencies in theoretical concepts as well as in generally accepted agreements for operating processes and quality standards for practical work. This seems especially obvious when one compares the present situation in Germany with Great Britain, The Netherlands or the United States. The view from the inside allows a differentiated consideration of the status quo and possible needs for change.

The pluralistic situation in Germany does not necessarily lead to disadvantages to the archaeological heritage. Though it is of crucial importance that archaeologists arrange things with each other in all cases where there is a need for similar ways of acting, especially in strategic questions of monument protection and care related to planning. Railway and motorway construction, as well as water regulation and the superordinated EIA should be treated (different from the existing situation) in the same way in all federal states.

German archaeology should also become more 'holistic'. Private enterprise should be accepted as part of the system. In turn, archaeological firms have to clarify their position and find their role between economic dependency as a contractor and scientific work within the framework of heritage management. Archaeological monument offices and archaeological companies should together broaden the existing written standards into specific guidelines, applicable to different activities and valid for all archaeological work carried out, whether carried out by a firm or a state office. The German State Archaeologists Committee should define the minimum financial level which ensures that archaeological investigations are of a high quality.

The biggest challenge for German archaeology in the near future will be the successful implementation of the Valletta Convention in times of high unemployment and with an empty treasury. Already politicians are asking for monument selection and ranking, with the aim of achieving a cost-saving *pars pro toto* monument preservation and research, which means to form a selection of monuments to preserve *in situ* or excavate, while the rest will be given up for destruction. Finding a solution to this problem will be far more difficult than all past assignments that German archaeology has faced.

References

Gumprecht, A. (2003) Der gesetzliche Rahmen für die Aufgaben der Bodendenkmalpflege in der Bundesrepublik Deutschland (BRD). In A. Wais and I. Oster (eds) *Archäologische Denkmalpflege in Deutschland,* 30–38. Stuttgart.

Horn, H. -G. (2003) Die Organisation der Bodendenkmalpflege. In Verband der Landesarchäologen in der Bundesrepublik Deutschland (eds) *Archäologische Denkmalpflege in Deutschland,* 39–44. Stuttgart.

N. N. (1998) Kommerzielle Archäologie *Archäologische Informationen* 21/22, 213–272.

Martin, D., J. N. Viebrock and R. Kleeberg (eds) (2005) *Deutsche Denkmalschutzgesetze.* (Schriftenreihe des Deutschen Nationalkomitees für Denkmalschutz 54, Auflage 4), Bonn.

Oebbecke, J. (ed.) (1997) *Privatisierung in der Bodendenkmalpflege: Öffentlich-rechtliche Fragen des Einsatzes privater Grabungsfirmen,* Baden-Baden.

CHAPTER 3

Quality management and Irish commercial sector archaeology

Margaret Gowen

Commercial archaeology is well established in Ireland after more than twenty years of growth and development. The commercial sector is currently engaged in very significant levels of licenced archaeological excavation and is also engaged at consultancy level with development planning and development-control related professional activity. Concern about the scale of excavation activity and an inadequate return to the published archaeological record has led to significant debate within the Irish archaeological profession which has intensified in recent years.

The problems, identified some years ago profession-wide, lie primarily with a widespread failure to achieve the conversion of a very significant body of technical survey and excavation reports, largely generated by commercial activity, into appropriately published and publicly accessible information. Furthermore, very little synthesised research has been undertaken using this data.

In this context, it is helpful to outline the history of the development of the commercial sector in Ireland in this context and to describe the nature of the state regulation of archaeological excavation activity. It is also important to describe how regulation is achieved and to describe the recent developments that have sought to achieve greater levels of quality control in commercial archaeology and greater dissemination of information.

LEGAL AND HISTORICAL BACKGROUND

The archaeological survey of Ireland commenced in the 1960s and saw a push to increase its coverage of the country in the 1980s. It progressed, as a paper survey, to the formation of a Sites and Monuments Record which was later called the Record of Monuments and Places (RMP). This inventory record became formally instated in National Monuments law in 1994 (Principal Act 1930; Amendments 1954, 1987 and 1994). Ireland has 120,000 recorded monuments and its historic towns have designated zones of archaeological potential.

The existence of the RMP forms the baseline of a system of information for development control and planning referral where monuments occur on or close to proposed development.

A parallel development occurred in the area of published government policy

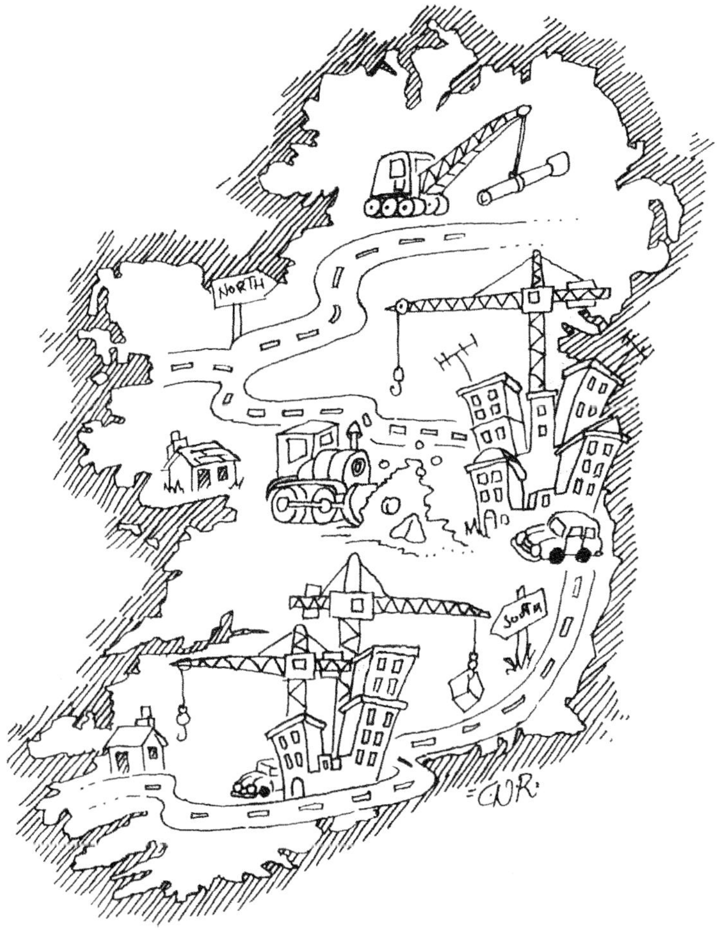

Figure 3.1 Busy Ireland.

(1999) and the ratification of the European Convention on the protection of the Archaeological Heritage (Valletta Convention signed 1992, ratified 1997). An important element of the policy document and the amended legislation passed at the time (National Monuments Amendment Act 1994, Heritage Act 1995) was the definition of what constitutes an archaeological monument in law.

The development of commercial sector activity

Starting in the 1980s and particularly from the latter half of the 1990s the 'Celtic Tiger' economy in Ireland fuelled an intensive and unprecedented level of infrastructural, private and public sector development (figure 3.1). This was facilitated and largely

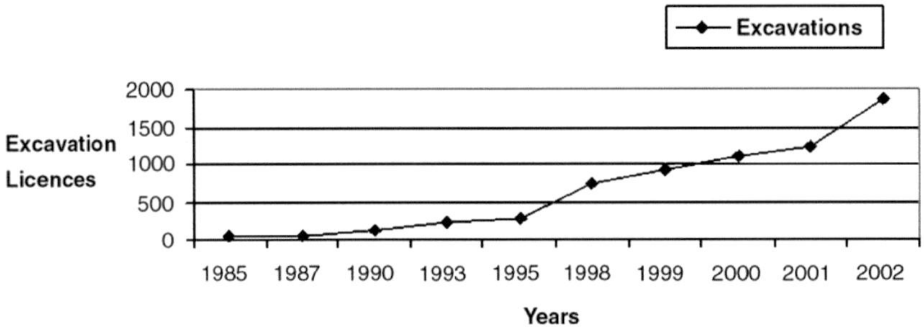

Figure 3.2 The licenced excavations in Ireland from 1985–2002.

augmented by generous European Union structural funding. This coupled with attractive tax incentives for particular types of private sector development the EU structural funds assisted Ireland in drafting and progressing a very ambitious National Development Plan 2000–2006, which will now probably extend to 2012.

The plan placed a particular emphasis on the need to develop the country's very inadequate infrastructure and particularly its roads network. Infrastructure development on such a comprehensive scale was bound to have a huge impact on archaeological sites and archaeological heritage management. The rapid development and growth of the already existing commercial sector in archaeology and cultural heritage management (CHM) was inevitable.

Initially, a small number of archaeological consultancy and contracting companies were formed, but the trends in demand generated by development were matched a growth in the profession. The level of increase in demand can be best illustrated by the growth in licensed archaeological excavation activity. For instance in 1990 there were 110 licensed excavations in the Republic of Ireland, up from 30 in 1974. The late 1990s brought significant growth and the sheer volume of physical construction led to a parallel development in commercial sector archaeological activity with the creation of many new companies, consultancies and contractor organisations. This development was market driven. It was neither anticipated, predetermined nor government-sponsored in any way. Most importantly, no one was prepared for the speed and scale of the growth in demand. The rapid growth which continued through the late 1990s is again best illustrated in the growth of numbers of licensed excavations which rose to 1050 in 2000 rising to 1800 by 2002 (figure 3.2). The commercial sector, by that time, represented 45% of all employed professional archaeologists (CHL Consulting Co. Ltd. 2002a; available at www.instituteofarchaeologistsofireland.ie). and that percentage has grown since then (figure 3.3).

For all involved, the situation was a 'fire fighting' response, with all sectors including the state services struggling to deal with a lack of resources. The management response has, however, became increasingly well-organised both at state level and in the realms

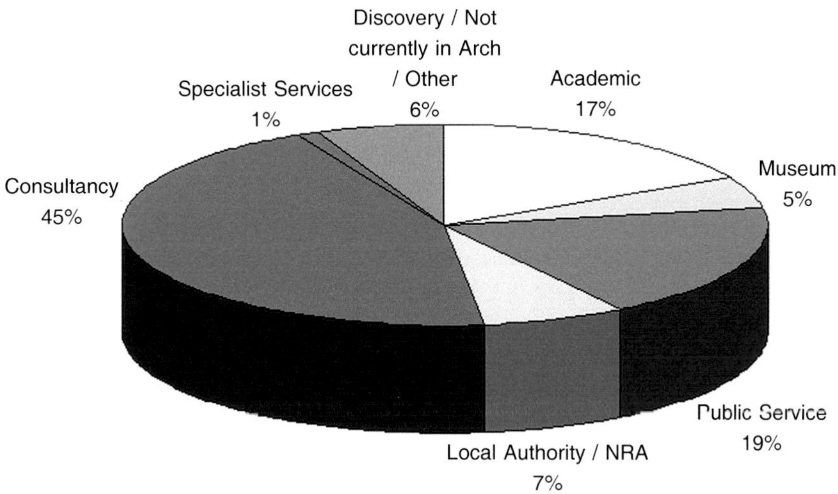

Figure 3.3 The sectors professional archaeologists were employed in, in 2002. (Data taken from CHL survey of Irish archaeological profession).

of the commercial activity, notwithstanding the dissolution in 2001 of the government department which had been created for the management of Arts, Heritage, Gaeltacht and the Islands. This was coupled with the dissolution, soon afterwards in 2002, of the State Heritage Service, Dúchas, the brand of which was seen in some political circles as 'anti-development'. The rationale presented by government at the time suggested that the change was sought in order to ensure that state management of heritage and archaeology would be more 'firmly bedded down' with state policy and brought into line with the government department that regulates planning, environment, local government and development control.

STATE REGULATION AND LICENSING

Irish national monuments legislation provides a legal framework governing the protection of monuments and sites and incorporates a requirement for the licensing of archaeological excavation. The licensing system, originally established in the primary National Monuments Act 1930, ensures prior notification and state approval of every single archaeological intervention and investigation of an invasive nature. It includes all proposed archaeological excavations including all test excavations for archaeological appraisal and development impact assessment purposes. Licensing also applies to situations where archaeological monitoring of development works may lead to a requirement for archaeological excavation.

In the 1987 legislation was also formulated and enacted in an amendment to the national Monuments Acts to ensure that the unregulated use of detection devices such as metal detectors would be made illegal. It is now illegal to use these devices for the purpose for recovering archaeological objects. Linked to this requirement is a requirement that all geophysical prospection and detailed surveys are also licensed.

In 2004 an amendment to the National Monuments Act, brought about an alternation in the licensing system with different types of permissions being granted for specific types of work, with a notable provision made for the management of the works associated with the National Plan. Road schemes, in particular, are now governed by a new system of control, governed by project-specific Ministerial Direction and monitored by the National Roads Authority Project Archaeologists (see O'Rourke, this volume). The approach, however, is essentially no different.

The regulations and procedures attaching to the legal framework have overseen significant developments in professional methods, technical processes, data gathering and the mandatory technical reporting of all Irish archaeological excavation activity. Moreover, the licensing system ensures a record of all excavations undertaken.

Quality control of post-excavation analysis and reporting, which should constitute a fully interpreted, culturally contexted archaeological record is, however, a much more difficult issue and one that the Irish profession is seeking to get to grips with. Whereas excavation activity in the field is both regulated and licensed, the quality of the outcome – the technical reports on the excavations – was neither strictly monitored or controlled, particularly with reference to research and further integrated analysis.

Many archaeologists must depend on voluntary, self motivated efforts to publish and seek peer review. There is no mandatory or secure overall structure for these publication efforts and no integrated framework for archaeological knowledge-building. Furthermore, there is no mechanism for archaeological information-based quality control on the technical reports that are submitted.

Successes can, nonetheless, be demonstrated. There are some very high quality publication outlets and there is increasing provision of grants for publication. An annual excavations bulletin, with summary accounts of all excavations conducted the previous year has been in publication since 1972. Peer review journals together with local archaeological and historical journals remain consistent in their output of archaeological publications. There has been very successful popular magazine-based publication in the quarterly 'Archaeology Ireland'. More recently, there has been significant development in the publication/presentation output of the National Roads Authority. Furthermore the past ten-fifteen years has seen the growth and development of independent, but nonetheless secure research frameworks for Irish urban archaeology with local authority assistance for publication. Also some important and useful research has emerged from large-scale development-led commercial projects.

However, relative to the overall volume of excavation activity these still remain too few in number. A study entitled 'Unpublished Excavations Survey 1930–1997', undertaken by the Heritage Council revealed that 43% had been published (Doyle *et al*. 2002, 9). The scale and volume of excavation activity has increased dramatically since that date and the trend in the ratio of published to unpublished reports noted in this survey (*ibid.*, 33) was one of increasing divergence.

Method Statements

In order to address this concern about the quality of the activity and the outcome, all applications for licences have had to be supported by detailed Method Statements since the mid 1990s. Method statements have to set out the type of site or sites in which the work is to be undertaken, detail about the proposed approach to excavation. These also have to:

- set out and provide details that illustrate the location, nature and extent of the proposed work;
- support the application with appropriate scaled maps and drawings;
- describe the proposed duration;
- describe the context in which the work is being carried out and for what purpose (for instance, if it is development-related – as is so often the case now in Ireland – the planning reference or development reference is quoted etc.).

LICENCE ELIGIBILITY

Twenty years ago licence eligibility was awarded on the basis of *curriculum vitae* and experience. In recent years the award of licence eligibility has been the subject of a more rigorous process of examination and interview by a professional board. The interview is conducted on behalf of the State archaeological service. A 'curriculum' for this qualification was set out some years ago and seminars were held, at the time, to inform and guide those seeking to apply. These however, did not continue and no formal curriculum has been put in place since that time. Recent developments and changes in the terms of reference for adjudicating suitability for licence eligibility, involving a loss of emphasis on academic qualification, led to much debate. There were significant differences of opinion within the profession and the decision generated grave disquiet among academic archaeologists. The change involved the removal of specific credits or marks awarded for academic experience, notably MA, M.Phil, M.Litt and PhD qualifications, with a more open adjudicating response to the inclusion of other forms of these kinds of third level training, together with a requirement for a demonstrable knowledge of Irish archaeology and an emphasis on practical excavation and post-excavation analysis experience. The change was seen by many as a retrograde step with undue importance placed on technical and methodological excavation ability.

An important feature of the licence, especially in this context, is that it is vested solely in the individual excavation director who, strictly speaking, carries sole responsibility for the report and published outcome. This can – and does – lead to a situation where quality becomes an individual matter or one that, in the commercial sector, can only be dealt with in the realms of employer advocacy and individual company policy and standards.

Reports and reporting

The licence awarded for any excavation carries with it an obligation to prepare and present a summary published report and to submit a full report. The quality of these reports has never been formally regulated, though guidelines have been developed. They remain, nonetheless, to a very large extent, technical reports. Reflecting the trends within the profession worldwide, the developments of recent years have led to a great corpus of 'grey literature' in Ireland. Attention is currently being given to the need to further assess the content and quality of this corpus, to provide a means of both publishing appropriate elements of it and to providing access to the information held within it.

Licensing tends to isolate the conduct and results of individual procedures. It can also, therefore, isolate licensees. The system, grounded in the technical Method Statement and the requirement of the licence to file a report with the National Monuments Service, can tend to devolve responsibility for research, publication and the integration of results from those funding (and sometimes managing) excavation projects, as the licence is held by the individual excavation directors. Furthermore, the filing of the technical report – a requirement of planning control – tends to be seen as an end in itself.

Following the important study commissioned by the Heritage Council on unpublished excavations referred to above, further study and discussion on potential methods of publication and dissemination have included the preparation of a Feasibility Study on the potential for the 'publication' of all the reports submitted to the state archaeological service at the Department of the Environment Heritage and Local Government. Since submission of a report is a mandatory requirement of licensing, it is felt that the quality of the reports submitted should be regulated by the department. The study suggests that placing these reports on the web would constitute a form of publication and would certainly lead to open access. It is widely felt that publication of all reports on the web should have a potent self-regulating effect on the quality and content of what is submitted, and that it should lead to a greater adherence to guidelines on report structure and content. Concern has been expressed in some sectors of the profession that early publication of technical reports could lead to issues of intellectual copyright; the licence holder/excavation director holds copyright. Technical reports are often not ready for formal peer review publication as the results and specialist analyses are not fully integrated into current research. The need for greater integration between the academic sector and the commercial sector will have a significant bearing on the quality of the outcome. It is hoped that significant dialogue, currently under way within the profession, together with the recent development of a continuing professional development programme by the Institute of Archaeologists of Ireland will address this issue and allay the concerns of those that do not support such a publication/presentation format.

The very active debate on this proposal in 2005 within the Heritage Council's Standing Committee on Archaeology and a dedicated committee sponsored by the Royal Irish Academy was further supported by an important University College Dublin-sponsored forum and Foresight Study in 2005 on the direction of the profession for the next 10 to 20 years. This study, entitled 'Archaeology 2020' was published in spring 2006 (University College Dublin 2006) and will now be followed by further structured discussion within the profession, assisted by the Royal Irish Academy.

OTHER DEVELOPMENTS IN QUALITY CONTROL

In the past, the development of a culture of professional responsibility in relation to publication and dissemination was left, in a very poorly resourced and funded environment, as a matter to be addressed by individuals. Elsewhere advocacy on professional standards came from a variety of quarters.

The Irish Association of Professional Archaeologists (IAPA) was established in the early 1970s. Its first two applications for membership from 'contract archaeologists' was hotly debated in 1986. These professionals were nonetheless admitted in a climate where the growth of commercial sector activity was neither sponsored or supported by the state, but simply arose as a response to lack of capacity within the State services to deal with a growing level of development and construction. Commercial sector activity was largely distrusted and isolated as a consequence.

Membership of IAPA, as it was then called, increased rapidly, with membership growing from well under 100 in the late 1970s and early 1980s to over 150 by the mid 1980s and with a present membership of around 350. The growth was attended by the development of a Code of Ethics, and a group of policy papers on professional practice which resulted in the adoption, by members, of a Code of Conduct. The development of this Association to more formal professional Institute status was long researched and discussed among members. The change and development was a singular achievement, lead by Maurice Hurley then City Archaeologist in Cork, who was chairman at the time.

Professional development, continuing training and the development of a culture of 'corporate responsibility' in relation to matters of publication and dissemination within the commercial sector was left as an issue to be addressed, as well as possible, within commercial activity. This left individuals seeking grant funding, companies seeking opportunity with commercial clients where possible and the development of publication policy as an issue to be addressed 'in house' by commercial companies.

The professional climate was such that there was a perception that commercial sector funding for such activity should not be an issue for those involved. However, it was a singular issue as development control, licensing and legislative requirements are not specific enough in relation to publication. This has also remained a critical issue for development sector commercial clients (those promoting and funding development) who perceive that they have no responsibility for what is regarded as an academic matter. Commercial clients frequently link publication of archaeological excavations with high end academic research, or they take the view that it is unnecessary expenditure on an outcome that may have limited public appeal or return to them. In other words they see no stakeholding in publication. The commercial client focus remains on the removal of the archaeological 'problem', so that construction can commence, and not on what happens to the data and the record thereafter.

INSTITUTE OF ARCHAEOLOGISTS OF IRELAND

The Institute of Archaeologists of Ireland (IAI), as it is now known, has moved to establish a greater emphasis on professional standards and self-regulation – and has further developed the IAPA Codes of Practice into a new set of Codes of Conduct which were adopted at the Institute's annual general meeting of 2006. IAI has also taken over the annual publication of the peer-reviewed 'Journal of Irish Archaeology'. In a parallel development, and with the Irish Heritage Council's assistance, IAI commissioned a study on the profile of the profession. This was undertaken in 2001–2003 and led to further studies in 2002–2003 on professional training needs analyses (CHL Consulting Co. Ltd., 2002b; available at www.instituteofarchaeologistsofireland.ie).

The results, in turn, led to the Institute's first steps towards the incorporation of a formal Continuing Professional Development programme. The studies resulted in the very welcome interest and help of the universities and other senior members of the profession and the Institute put its first 'Pilot Programme' in place in 2006 along with steps towards the adoption of a formal method of accreditation.

Discussion has taken place between the IAI and the government on the potential for higher levels of self regulation within the profession. As matters stands at present, however, the licensing system remains, and will remain, as an important cornerstone of regulation, control and the tracking of excavation activity while the Institute is currently focusing on raising standards though guidance and, in time, a set of fully instated, mandatory standards and accredited continuing professional education and training for its members.

The Heritage Council

The Heritage Council continues to assist the profession greatly by commissioning

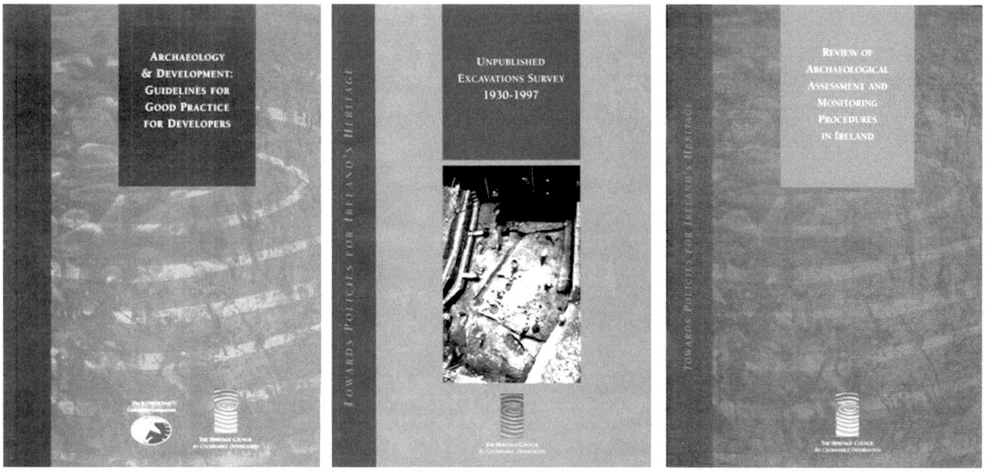

Figure 3.4 Studies commissioned by the Heritage Council that have analysed various aspects of Irish archaeology.

studies that facilitate the numeric and qualitative analysis of a whole range of issues for archaeology. These include studies on: unpublished excavations; research in urban archaeology; standards of practice in urban archaeology; archiving of excavation records; monuments at risk; grading archaeological monuments; reuse of churches and graveyards; aerial archaeology; landscape characterisation (figure 3.4) (for the full range of Heritage Council Studies on archaeology see www.heritagecouncil.ie/archaeology. All this has occurred with a parallel provision from the Council for generous grant funding for the publication of individual projects of archaeological research and for the publication of excavation results.

NATIONAL ROADS AUTHORITY

Increased levels of construction activity in recent years, especially in relation to the National Development Plan and road-building, have led to a number of other welcome developments. One of the most important of these is the formal archaeological management in house, by the National Roads Authority (NRA), of the vast amounts of archaeological excavation being generated by road building in Ireland. This move was preceded by the preparation of a Code of Practice between the NRA and the State Department (figure 3.5) (for an example of the document see www.nra.ie/archaeology). It was followed soon afterwards by the preparation of similar codes between the State Heritage Service and other bodies responsible for large scale development and the provision of infrastructure. These included:

Bord Gáis, the Irish gas board; Coillte, the Irish forestry service; and the Irish Concrete Federation (sand and gravel extraction and quarrying). From the perspective of this paper, these codes and their provisions ensure that excavation activity is monitored by project archaeologists employed by the commissioning agency/authority with the codes placing an emphasis on the responsibility for dissemination of the results of archaeological work. Real progress has been made in this regard with NRA roads projects through web-based presentation of all technical reports, the publication of summary information sheets, public lectures and seminars and the preparation of technical guidance documents.

Figure 3.5 A good example of archaeological management: a Code of Practice between the government and the National Roads Authority.

SELF REGULATION IN THE COMMERCIAL SECTOR

Commercial activity by its nature is competitive and market driven. Commercial reputation is both achieved and maintained through the achievement of high standards, accurate information and high quality presentation. The Irish commercial sector has had to professionalise its activity in order to provide a coherent professional response to the demands of Ireland's rapidly developing economy and its enormous construction industry.

However, as a service, its client base has little or no perception of a stakeholding in the quality of its end product, which has to be a secure return to archaeological knowledge. As mentioned above, internal mechanisms for quality control are largely a matter for each company. In some instances ISO quality standards are incorporated into management processes. The company culture, however, governs and influences the commitment to quality. Companies often provide structured in house training, especially for fieldwork (figure 3.6). However, the creation of research frameworks, management review, in house peer review of reports and the preparation of papers monographs and books for publication and a focus on dissemination through the web and other media is very much a discretionary matter. It has been found that it can take considerable time and a consistent level of significant commercial activity for any company to mature to a point where it can achieve this and can

Figure 3.6 As the mechanisms for quality control are largely a matter for each company, they often provide structured in house training, especially for fieldwork.

securely identify research themes arising from its own work or an interface with existing research frameworks (notably in cities and towns). Furthermore, it can be difficult in an intensely competitive environment to create opportunities for research within projects and to resource staff appropriately during post-excavation report preparation for high quality publication with sufficient research content.

CONCLUSIONS

Issues relating to the quality of archaeological work and its output have been very actively addressed by the archaeological profession in Ireland in recent years, with the level of debate accelerating in 2005–2006. However, no clear framework or structure has yet been devised for achieving higher desired levels of information quality control and knowledge building through publication and wider dissemination of the results of archaeological excavation activity and research. Access to data is clearly not enough, although the proposed web-based publication of all technical reports could improve the situation greatly. It is obvious that far greater professional integration is required – between the state regulatory and heritage management services, the universities, the National Museum, the Institute of Archaeologists of Ireland, the dedicated research institutions and the state-sponsored and commercial sectors. In the first instance, the analysis of the current situation needs to be brought to a conclusion. Only then will the necessary values be articulated and the necessary peer review structures be put in place that can provide professional confidence. The challenge is to ensure a far greater emphasis on the quality of culturally integrated archaeological knowledge with a recognised value for Irish society.

References

CHL Consulting Co. Ltd. (2002a) *The Future Demand for Archaeologists in Ireland.* (Unpublished report for The Heritage Council and the Institute of Archaeologists of Ireland). Dublin.

CHL Consulting Co. Ltd. (2002b) *Profile of the Archaeological Profession and Education Resources in Ireland.* (Unpublished report for The Heritage Council and the Institute of Archaeologists of Ireland). Dublin.

Doyle, I. W., D. Jennings and J. MacDermott (2002) *Unpublished Excavations in the Republic of Ireland 1930–1997.* Dublin.

University College Dublin (2006) *Archaeology 2020. Repositioning Irish Archaeology in the Knowledge Society: A realistically achievable perspective.* Dublin.

CHAPTER 4

Quaestors, quality and quantity: archaeology and the National Roads Authority in Ireland

Dáire O'Rourke

INTRODUCTION

The Irish National Roads Authority (NRA) was established in 1994 following a legislative change with the 1993 Roads Act. The Authority was set up as an independent body but has a relationship with the Department of Transport. The primary function of the National Roads Authority is 'to secure the provision of a safe and efficient network of national roads'. This is done with the NRA as funding agent and the work is carried out by consultants and contractors employed through road design offices attached to the local authorities nationwide. There are 14 such road design offices around the country and each office looks after the national road network in their catchment area. Where a new road impacts on a number of different counties, one county becomes the leading authority and *de facto* in charge of that section of new road. The NRA is, in effect, the funding agency with over-arching responsibility for the roads programme, but the day-to-day responsibility of individual road building lies with the local authorities.

The national road-building programme is one of the most ambitious projects being undertaken by the Irish Government. Years of infrastructural neglect had meant that Ireland's roads and bridges were sub standard and unable to meet the needs of a growing and vibrant economy. The National Development Plan launched in 2000 and set to last until 2006, saw the development of Ireland's infrastructure to be a major factor. Plans for new motorways and the upgrading of existing roads were formulated and agreed in principle and form a crucial part of the National Development Plan.

This major investment in Ireland's infrastructure has meant that many new roads are being built in rural areas. Ireland's main economy for years was agriculture and the country was never part of any major industrial revolution. While there are a number of major cities and towns, Irelands' settlement pattern is largely rural and dispersed. This has ensured that archaeological sites and monuments have pervaded through the centuries (figure 4.1). There are over 170,000 known or recorded archaeological monuments in Ireland. These are sites that have been identified by the surveys conducted by the State Archaeological Service. However, many archaeological sites have no proper surface expression and are not visible to the naked eye. Thus the 170,000 known monuments are seen as being merely the

Figure 4.1 A 45m souterrain under excavation at Newtownbalregan on the M1 Dundalk Western Bypass.

tip of the iceberg. This was identified by the National Monuments Service and by the National Roads Authority as being an issue in relation to the development of the roads programme in an archaeologically rich environment.

CODE OF PRACTICE

Archaeology was seen as a major impact in the national road-building programme, so these two bodies took a pro-active stance and in 2000 a Code of Practice was agreed (NRA and DAHGI 2000). The code was agreed between the National Roads Authority and the Minister for Arts, Heritage, Gaeltacht and the Islands (then the Minister tasked with the care of Ireland's archaeological heritage). The purpose of the code is 'to provide a framework within existing legislation and policies to enable the national Roads Authority to progress with its programme of work within the timescale of the national Development Plan whilst carrying appropriate archaeological mitigation having regard to a set of principles and actions agreed by both parties.'

It outlines a number of guiding principles recognising that the State Archaeological Service has a responsibility to protect the archaeological heritage and the NRA has the responsibility to secure the provision of a safe and efficient network of national roads. As there is the potential there for conflict, a partnership approach was adopted between the State Archaeological Service and the National Roads Authority. Aligned to *the developer pays principle* the NRA agreed to finance a balanced and cost effective approach to archaeological investigation, excavation and mitigation as an integral element of road project costs. The NRA must also strive to avoid direct impacts on archaeology, taking account of road design and safety implications, environmental and other impacts and costs.

In real terms the code was quite revolutionary in that it saw the developer, the National Roads Authority, employ their own archaeologists, directly and through the local authorities. The archaeologists employed by the local authorities are called Project Archaeologists, who manage the archaeological aspects of road schemes from the planning stages to the on site stages, post excavation stages and finally to publication. The application of the code by the NRA is demonstrated by the employment of four archaeologists directly and twenty-one project and assistant archaeologists appointed to the road design offices associated with the local authorities nationwide. There are currently 14 road design offices nationwide in Ireland, of which all bar one have one or more project and assistant archaeologists working solely on the archaeological aspects of the national road-building programme.

Project archaeologists

The NRA's archaeology policy and strategy has been devised by the Authority's archaeology section, while paying due regard to national and EU legislation and policy documents. The project archaeologists are a key element in the Authority's archaeology policy and are also essential to implementing its archaeology strategy. This policy is avoidance where possible of known archaeological sites and to provide a comprehensive and coherent strategy in relation to the archaeological investigation and mitigation of sites where this is not possible. When first introduced

Figure 4.2 The organisational structure of the NRA archaeology section.

it was the first time in Ireland where such a whole scale move was implemented. Archaeologists, now working directly for the developer were part of the design team and part of every aspect of the decision making process from the planning stages to the on site works. The primary role of the Project Archaeologist is to manage the archaeological process on behalf of the local authority/NRA. This involves ensuring that risks are minimised in relation to archaeology and to ensure that best archaeological practices and standards are employed. Their role involves the procurement of private archaeological companies to carryout the initial landscape study phases and the preparation of contract specifications for all aspects of the work. They must also oversee the on-site testing and excavation stages and the off-site post excavation stages. It is also their responsibility to ensure the scheme is brought to publication.

While the Project and Assistant Project Archaeologists are located in the road design offices associated with the local authorities nationwide, the National Roads Authority funds their positions. This structure (see figure 4.2), which has fluidity and flexibility, ensures that the project archaeologists are on the ground and managing the archaeological aspects of the road schemes in their areas. Dealing with a dispersed team, located in different parts of the country and in different local councils, is not always simple and such a fluid arrangement is not without problems. To countenance this and to attempt to streamline the approach to archaeology, a number of guidelines have been issued.

GUIDELINES

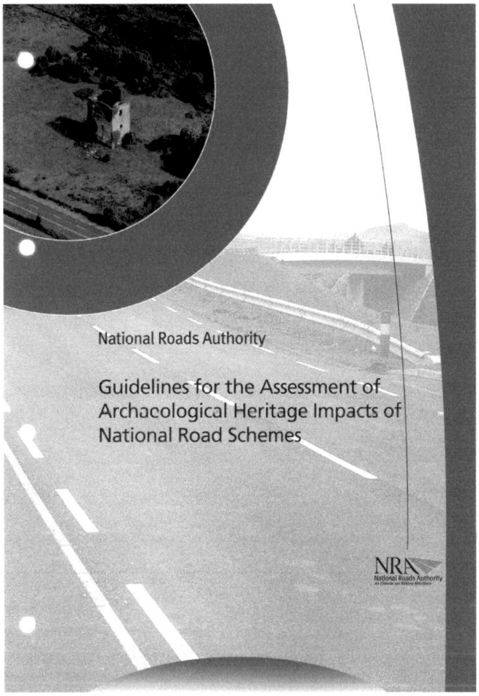

Figure 4.3 In 2006 the NRA launched Guidelines for the Assessment of Archaeological Heritage Impacts of National Road Schemes.

To ensure this consistency of approach and to ensure that the maximum non-invasive landscape interrogation occurs at the planning stage a new set of guidelines, titled Guidelines for the Assessment of Archaeological Heritage Impact of National Road Schemes, was launched in early 2006 (figure 4.3). Similar guidelines were also launched in relation to the architectural heritage and it is intended that both sets of guidelines be read and used in tandem where appropriate. The guidelines have been formulated taking due cognisance of National, European and International guidances and legislation. They are the first of their kind in Ireland in relation to archaeology and form part of a suite of guideline documents in relation to the broader issues of environmental assessment in the planning stages. The archaeology guidelines mirror the National Road Project Management Guidelines (NRPMG) formulated by the NRA. The NRPMG outline the procedures to be followed by the NRA and local authorities in the planning, design and implementation of road schemes as set out in legislation. The road planning process involves three main stages: a Constraints Study, a Route Corridor Selection Study, and a Environmental Impact Statement. Archaeology is a major factor in these three aspects of the planning process.

The Constraints Study

The Constraints Study Area identifies a large geographical area where a new road or motorway is required. Data collection at this point is desk based and includes the identification of all recorded archaeological monuments within the study area, including their legal status. It forms the baseline from which further studies emanate (see for example Courtney and Gowen 1999).

The Route Corridor Selection Study

The Route Corridor Selection Study involves the identification of a number of broad route corridor options. These corridors are the length of the required road/motorway and up to several hundred meters in width. This study augments the Constraints Study by expanding on the desk-based information but also conducting site visits and aerial inspection. A crucial aspect of this survey is an impact assessment of the route options. Within these broad route corridors potential route options emerge. It is often possible at this stage to adjust the route to avoid known archaeological sites and thus minimise the archaeological risk (see for example Kilfeather 2000).

The Environmental Impact Statement

The Environmental Impact Statement (EIS) phase of the planning process is to assess the impact of the national road schemes on the archaeological heritage. This study builds on the work already collated during the previous planning stages. The EIS focuses on the preferred route and allows this route to be studied in greater detail. As well as further desk-based research, detailed field inspection and aerial survey is also carried out. Specialist surveys (including topographical survey or geophysical survey etc.) are often carried out on specific areas, if deemed appropriate at this stage. This part of the study will also include a description of the receiving archaeological environment, a comprehensive (as possible) site inventory, identification of landscapes of archaeological potential and a statement of archaeological impact with mitigation measures (for example, the M3 Scheme consists of seven volumes).

The EIS is a very important document for it must encapsulate the impact that the new road will have on the environment. It is imperative that the archaeology section of the EIS identifies as clearly as possible both the known sites and monuments and their landscape setting as well as the potential archaeological sites and monuments and their landscape setting. The archaeological landscape must be mapped as part of this process and a comprehensive methodology applied to ensure the optimum level of information is received recorded and presented so that the planning process is informed in a thorough fashion. It is imperative that the EIS include a full and comprehensive desk-study; results of detailed field inspection; results of aerial survey; results of specialist survey (if carried out); full description of sites (previously known and newly discovered); full consideration and cross referencing of monuments; full consideration of archaeological potential of the landscape; full consideration of archaeological potential of wetlands and rivers; full impact assessment of the preferred route option; full consideration of proposed mitigation measures; and details of consultation with landowners, the State archaeological service, architectural heritage consultant and the Project Archaeologist and road design team. The EIS once published is then submitted for decision at the independent planning board.

Each aspect of the guidelines, *i.e.* the Constraints Study, Route Corridor Selection

Study and the EIS all contain a checklist at the end of each section to ensure that all relevant information has been compiled and included.

The purpose of the guidelines is to provide guidance on the treatment of the archaeological heritage during the planning and design of road schemes. The guidelines also play an important role in ensuring a comprehensive and consistent approach is brought to bear in relation to the archaeological aspects of road schemes at the planning stage.

For the on-site phases of the archaeological work, one of the biggest challenges lay in relation to wetland sites. Wetland archaeology and the potential for wetland archaeology were being seen as a stumbling block to advance investigation and mitigation of sites. A somewhat *ad hoc* approach was being employed and wetland areas were being omitted from the advance archaeological works. This was a very unsatisfactory situation and so it was deemed crucial to produce guidelines for this milieu.

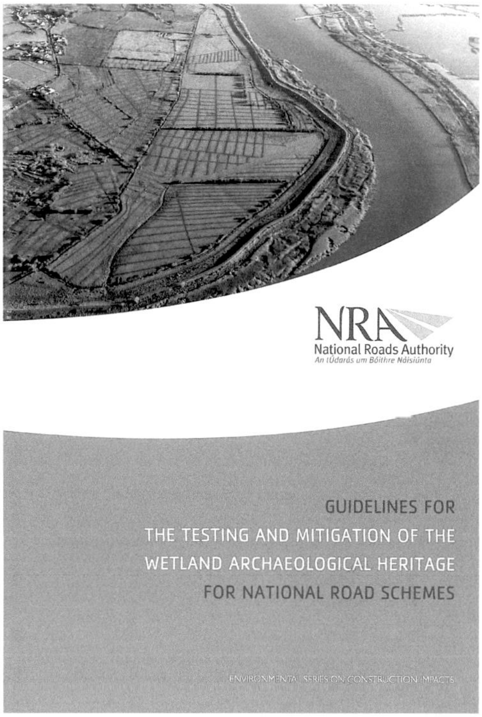

Figure 4.4 In 2006 the NRA launched Guidelines for the Testing and Mitigation of the Wetland Archaeological Heritage for National Road Schemes.

Early in 2006, the Guidelines for the Testing and Mitigation of the Wetland Archaeological Heritage for National Road Schemes were launched (figure 4.4). These guidelines are intended to assist the road project design team, project archaeologist, archaeological consultants and contractors working on archaeological testing, field survey, excavation and post excavation phases of archaeological mitigation on national road schemes. The guidelines outline a range of general recommendations that need to be considered in approaching archaeological work in wetland environments, a range of practical approaches relevant to both assessment and excavation and a select bibliography offering comparative methodologies, applied in both Ireland and Britain to projects in wetland environments. They have succeeded in demystifying the practical work required in relation to wetland archaeology and also added to the streamlining of archaeology and roads.

A number of other archaeological guidelines are in the pipeline. The most imminent deals with the use of geophysical survey as part of the planning process in advance of a new road and also during the on site phases as part of site investigations. The use of geophysics within archaeological contexts was pioneered in Ireland by the state funded research body, the Discovery Programme, principally in the work on Tara (see Newman 1997). However, it has been used more and more as an investigation tool, coupled with trial trenching as part of the advanced archaeological work as part of the roads programme. However, fears that it was not being used efficiently or effectively, have led to the development of these guidelines.

The range of topics to be addressed in these forthcoming guidelines include; survey environments (terrestrial urban, terrestrial rural, alluvium and colluvium, wetland, rivers and lakes, intertidal, marine); survey control, layout and navigation (total station, differential GPS); terrestrial survey techniques (magnetometry, magnetic gradient, total field, magnetic susceptibility, electrical resistance, ground penetrating radar and electrical resistivity tomography, topography, micro-topography, airborne LIDAR); electromagnetics (metal detecting, soil electrical conductivity, seismics, gravity, airborne remote sensing); waterborne survey techniques, (bathymetry, single beam sonar, multibeam sonar, sidescan sonar, sub-bottom profiler); and other techniques such as metal detecting. The guidelines will also deal with project design, survey specification and project management, quality control, survey practice, data processing and presentation, compatibility with subsequent archaeological testing requirements, analysis/interpretation, reporting, and compatibility with subsequent archaeological testing requirements. There will also be a glossary and select bibliography. The aim of these guidelines is to identify strategies for situations in which geophysical survey can be used, to identify the types of archaeological features that may be located using geophysical techniques (figure 4.5) and to identify non-archaeological factors that may influence the response or sensitivity of geophysical techniques. The guidelines for conducting geophysical investigations for archaeology in relation to road schemes are to be launched in 2006.

PROCUREMENT

The primary reason that we have standards and guidances is to ensure a consistency of approach and a quality product at the end of the process. The Code of Practice, as outlined above, facilitated the provision for Project Archaeologists to manage the archaeological aspects of Ireland's national road schemes. However, the archaeological work is carried out by archaeological consultants, in relation to the planning phase and archaeological contractors in relation to the on-site investigation and excavation phases. Since the Code of Practice was agreed in 2000 and the NRA began employing archaeologists it is now policy to employ archaeological contractors and consultants using EU procurement procedures. All archaeological work above the thresholds required are advertised in the European Union Journal (EUJ) and most other archaeological work too. Work is procured through the EU Directives, using Common Procurement Vocabulary (CPV) Codes. Prior to the NRA procuring archaeological companies this way, no CPV codes existed for

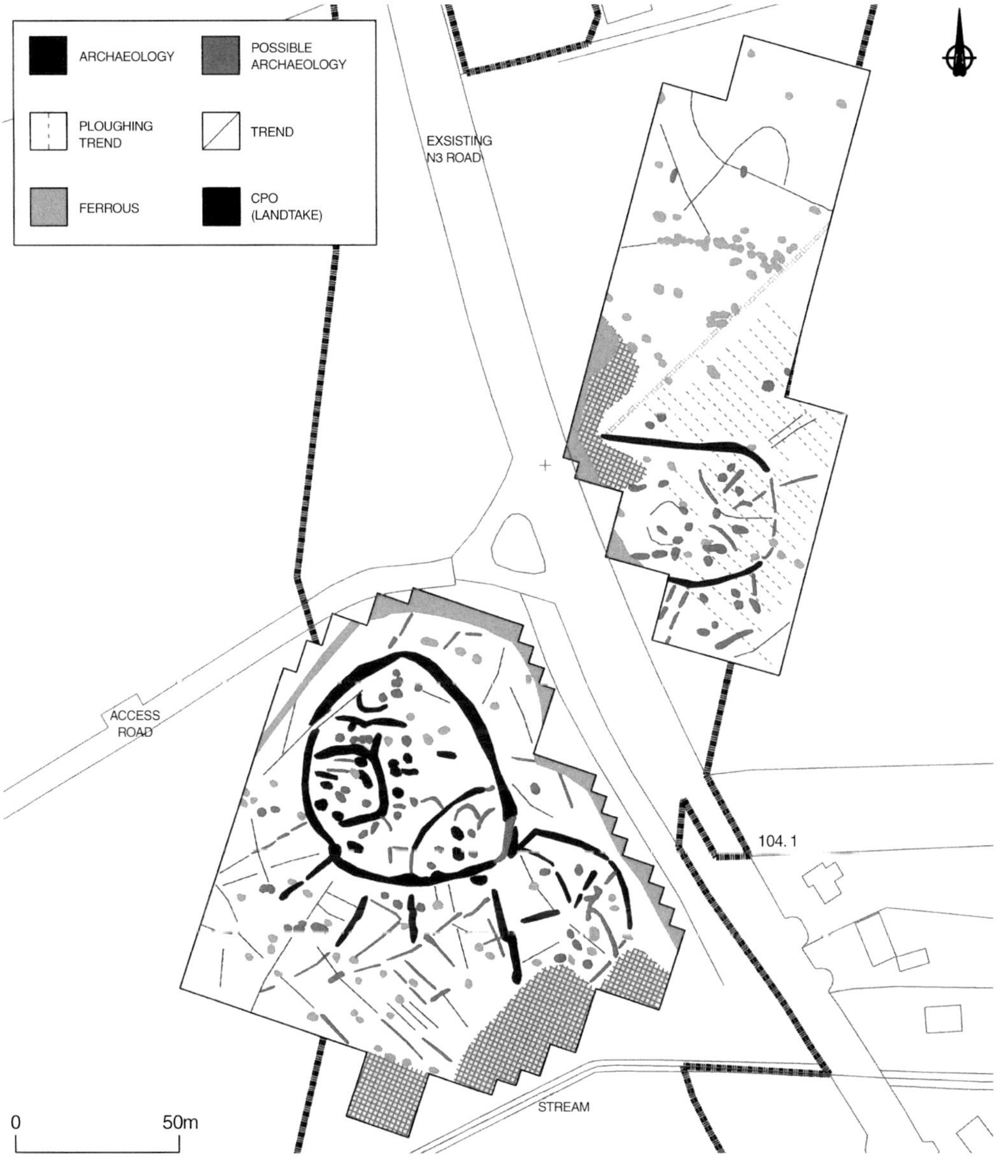

Figure 4.5 Enclosure complex as revealed by geophysical survey and testing at Roestown, County Meath in advance of the M3 Clonee-North of Kells Motorway Scheme (Figure GSB Prospection & ACS Ltd).

archaeology. The NRA requested the creation of such codes from the EU and is responsible for the creation of CPV codes in relation to archaeological excavation, geophysical survey and topographical survey. Further CPV codes are currently being sought by the NRA in relation to archaeological excavation services (test excavation, excavation, monitoring), post excavation services (excavation reporting, specialist analyses, publication) and additional archaeological services (walk-over surveys, archaeological topographic survey, underwater survey, archaeo-geophysical survey, archaeological desk-top studies. The use of standard EU procurement procedures ensures competition for work, opens up the market place in Ireland for non-Irish companies and – by its nature – encourages a quality approach. It also provides our financial managers with a transparent approach to the procurement of archaeological services, the contracts of which are worth many millions of Euro annually. Transparency of approach and methodology is as useful a tool in encouraging a quality approach as any other.

QUALITY

Through the introduction of the code of practice and associated archaeological management structure, the publication of a number of guidances and the procurement of archaeological services through the EU procurement procedure, the NRA has attempted and succeeded in may ways in ensuring that archaeological work associated with road schemes in Ireland is carried out efficiently and in a standardised manner (figure 4.6). However, it is important to measure this approach and to ascertain the success or failure of various methodologies by looking at the end product. For many developers, engineers, etc. the product of archaeological investigation and excavation is the excavated site, the hole dug in the ground. They are happy when the site has been excavated and the way 'cleared' for the new road or office block. They are not concerned with the post excavation analysis or the dissemination of the information. For many, the quality of the work is not important. If the report is never written, they will not worry. For many archaeology is a nuisance, something to get rid of, as one may swat away a fly. Developers and engineers speak of value for money, which for some appears to be the 'cheapest price and the quickest job' with little or no regard for quality. However, thankfully this is no longer the case for the archaeology associated with the Irish national roads programme, in the majority of cases. It has been important to evaluate the term value for money when used in relation to archaeology and to apply criteria, which are compatible to archaeology so that the 'cheapest price quickest job' phenomenon does not have to apply in every case. Part of the criteria for value for money include methodologies employed, project efficiency, resources employed etc. However the most important of all these criteria is dissemination and how the archaeological data that is collected on site is transformed from information into knowledge. It is this output, the knowledge output, that is the true measure of any archaeological work.

The knowledge output is the product created as a result of all the archaeological work associated with the planning and design phases of the project, the on-site

Figure 4.6 Archaeologists working on the site of an early medieval vertical watermill uncovered during excavations at Killoteran, County Waterford in advance of construction of the N25 Waterford Bypass (Photo StudioLab).

advance investigation and excavation phases and the post excavation phases. To ensure that a quality product is created, and that the product is generated into information, which is generated into knowledge and subsequently disseminated is the true yard stick by which any archaeological work can be measured and deemed to be a success or a failure. It is the challenge we have set ourselves.

On conventional road schemes, the archaeological investigations, excavations and post excavation phases are followed by the site report. A number of our early schemes are just finishing post excavation and now are moving towards publication. It is planned that a number of publications pertaining to the archaeological work associated with road schemes will be published in 2007. To bring these schemes to fruition, and to provide a quality assurance to this work, a number of academic archaeologists have been retained to ensure that these publications are finalised. They in effect have a mentoring role and in some of the early schemes from 2000/2001 etc. the academics were only brought onto the project at the end of the post excavation phase. This is one way by which a quality approach is sought.

Ballyhanna Research Project

This need for a quality approach has been extended in more recent years. In 2001/2002 archaeological excavations as part of a new road in County Donegal in the north west of Ireland revealed a previously unknown medieval cemetery at Ballyhanna County Donegal, with over 1,000 articulated human skeletons *in situ* (figure 4.7). Rather than carry out the archaeological analysis of the skeletal remains as part of a conventional post excavation osteological study and report, the NRA and Donegal County Council (the local authority tasked with building the road) agreed to fund a research programme with two academic institutions, Queens University Belfast and the Institute of Technology in Sligo. The objective of this partnership approach is to apply the osteo-archaeological and scientific skills of the staff from both institutions to investigate the human bone assemblage from Ballyhanna, County Donegal, over a three-year period.

It is envisaged that this corpus of material has substantial research potential and will provide the opportunity for the development of a number of projects in the future. The research project involves the funding of two postgraduate degrees in the Institute of Technology Sligo, one in biomolecular archaeology and the other in archaeological chemistry. It also includes the funding of one doctorate in osteo-archaeology being awarded through Queens University Belfast. The Masters study in relation to biomolecular archaeology aims to determine whether there are ancient DNA sequences within the adult assemblages from Ballyhanna suitable for Polymerase Chain Reaction (PCR). PCR amplification will assist in the gender determination of juveniles and adults. The Masters study in archaeological chemistry involves the trace elemental analysis of archaeological bone using the techniques of Inductively Coupled Plasma – Mass Spectroscopy (ICP–MS), Graphite Furnace Atomic Absorption Spectrometry (GFAAS), Flame Atomic Absorption Spectrometry (FAAS) and Flame Atomic Emission Spectrometry (FAES). It is hoped that in the proposed study multi-element data for bone will provide baseline data for dietary and other inferences for the population under study. The results will provide baseline data to facilitate evaluation of dietary, social, environmental and toxicological factors affecting this population. The PhD in osteo-archaeology will involve the osteological and palaeo-pathological analysis of the adult remains. All adult individuals would be analysed for the purposes of ascertaining their age-at-death, sex and stature using standard osteological methodology. In addition, there will also be detailed analysis of any injuries or disease incurred during the lifetime of the individuals. Standard metrical and non-metrical information will also be recorded and this will potentially be made available to other postgraduate students for further projects. A research assistant position is also being funded to assist the project.

This approach was decided upon as a result of evaluating best value for money. The archaeological profession will benefit as a result of funding more post graduate positions and the NRA and local authority benefit from having a more in depth analysis of the material than perhaps a standard osteological report might allow.

Figure 4.7 Skeleton uncovered during excavations of a medieval burial ground at Ballyhanna, County Donegal in advance of construction of the N15 Bundoran-Ballyshannon bypass.

M3 RESEARCH FRAMEWORK

The Ballyhanna Bones Research Project, as it has become known, is a research project associated with one site from one road scheme. The next step was to look at a road scheme and to see if we could design a research framework to fit into the scheme. The opportunity arrived in the form of the M3, a road scheme that is one of the most controversial in the country. The M3 is the new motorway in County Meath in the east of Ireland, 60 km in length and covering approximately 700 hectares of land. The M3 road project has been dominated by the issue of the relationship the road will have to the Hill of Tara, 1.2 km away. Outside help was sought from a senior Irish academic in developing the M3 research framework. The research framework was devised once the investigative nature of the archaeological work was completed. Once the desktop survey, field survey, geophysical survey, aerial survey and extensive test excavation were carried out and 160 new archaeological sites were located along the length of the road, the framework was developed (figure 4.8). It comprises a three-pronged dimension. It is proposed to place the newly uncovered archaeological data into its archaeological, historical and palaeo-environmental context. This is being achieved by employing an academic archaeologist with a specific interest and experience in this geographical area, an historian and a palaeo-environmentalist who as well as advising on sampling strategies is looking at the wider archaeological landscape into which the new road will run. It is a very exciting project and one which is currently underway. The primary aim of the research framework is to maximise the research potential and to disseminate the results widely.

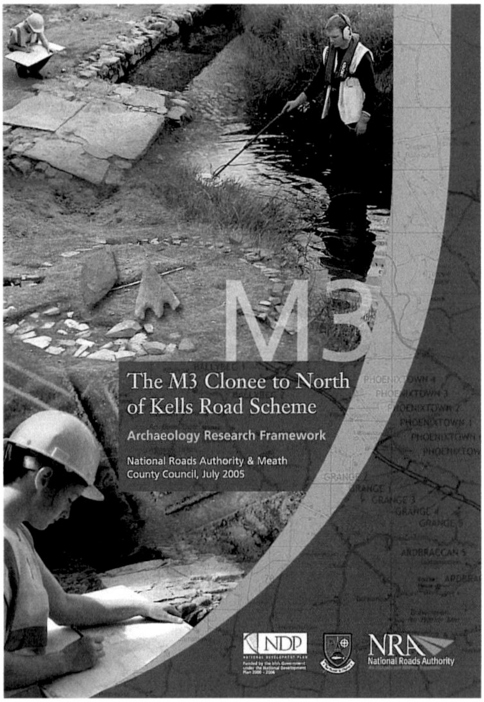

Figure 4.8 In 2005 the NRA and Meath County Council launched the M3 Clonee to North of Kells Road Scheme Archaeology Research Framework.

Post-doctoral fellowship in landscape archaeology

The information generated from the M3 research framework will feed into a larger research project currently being funded in the School of Archaeology University College Dublin. The post-doctoral fellowship has two main objectives; to assess the effectiveness of the NRA's archaeological policies in providing knowledge about Ireland's past through its archaeological heritage and to assess the character and significance of the wider archaeological landscapes impacted on by past, present and future NRA road projects.

The first aim will involve carrying out a full assessment of archaeological works on NRA road schemes, both current and recently completed. A comparison with archaeological mitigation on other European road projects will also be drawn. The study will then suggest any aspects for further archaeological development.

The second aim will involve an archaeological landscape study for a chosen study area(s) where Irish National Roads have been developed or improved. The aim will be to characterise a series of archaeological landscapes in order to assess the past, present and future implications of the roads building programme. A detailed case study will be undertaken on a territory of Ancient Meath. This area is crossed by parts of the M1, N2, M3, M4 and M50 road schemes. This work is due to commence in late 2006.

CONCLUSION

Ireland is currently going through an economic boom with an unprecedented level of investment in development and in infrastructure. From an archaeological viewpoint, this has an enormous impact on the visible and invisible archaeological landscapes that abound in the country. It is an amazing opportunity to explore our heritage and one, which should not be lost. The development of the Code of Practice in relation to archaeology between the National Roads Authority and the State Archaeological Service has released a dynamic impetus into the environment, with the employment of project archaeologists and for the first time in Ireland archaeologists project managing the archaeological impacts of national road schemes. The development of guidelines, coupled with the management structure in place due to the code of practice has sought to further standardise our approaches to archaeology. A standardised approach should ensure a quality of approach and a quality product at the end of the cycle. The onus is on us as archaeologists to ensure that the archaeological work being carried out is to the highest standard, that dissemination of the results is achieved, not just for the archaeological profession but also for the wider community as a whole. It is, I believe, also incumbent upon us as archaeologists to ensure value for money and a method to securing this is to think 'outside the box' and apply research frameworks to road schemes, to have a partnership approach with academic institutions and most importantly to ensure that this incredible opportunity which has been given to us to mitigate for archaeology in the Republic of Ireland is not wasted.

References

Courtney, L. and M. Gowen (1999) *Archaeological Constraints Study N3 Dunshaughlin-Navan.* (Unpublished report prepared for Meath County Council).

Kilfeather, A. (2000) '*N3 Navan to Dunshaughlin Route Selection Archaeology' contained in Section 2, Dunshaughlin to Navan, Halcrow Barry Consultant Engineers, September 2001.* (Unpublished report prepared for Meath County Council).

National Roads Authority (2005) *Guidelines for the Assessment of Archaeological Heritage Impacts of National Road Schemes.* Dublin.

National Roads Authority (2005) *Guidelines for the Assessment of Architectural Heritage Impacts of National Road Schemes.* Dublin.

National Roads Authority (2005) *Guidelines for the Testing and Mitigation of the Wetland Archaeological Heritage for National Road Schemes.* Dublin.

National Roads Authority and the Department of Arts, Heritage, Gaeltacht and the Islands (2000) *Code of Practice between the National Roads Authority and the Minister for Arts, Heritage, Gaeltacht and the Islands.* Dublin.

Newman, C. (1997) *Tara: An archaeological survey.* (Discovery Programme Monograph 2). Dublin.

CHAPTER 5

Quality assurance in archaeology, the Dutch perspective

Monique van den Dries and Willem Willems

INTRODUCTION

In the Netherlands quality assurance in archaeology is a rather new phenomenon. Until the late 1990s, a traditional system was maintained whereby the quality and relevance of archaeological investigation was thought to be sufficiently guaranteed by a very restrictive licensing system. Even under the revised Monuments Act of 1988, only universities, the State Archaeological Service (*Rijksdienst voor het Oudheidkundig bodemonderzoek*, ROB) and municipalities could obtain a licence to carry out excavations, apparently under the assumption that this restrictive access to excavation, in combination with some additional conditions, would guarantee the quality of the work.

A more explicit system of quality assurance was introduced in the late 1990s, after a change in government had led to a change of policy and a new Minister for Culture, trained as an economist, had decided that commercial archaeology would be the best way forward (see Willems 2005). The Dutch parliament passed a ratification act of the Malta Convention in 1998. This paved the path for commercial archaeology because the decision implied that the principles of the convention were formally recognised and were included in heritage policy.

In this paper, we will discuss the approach that was chosen in the Netherlands, the quality assurance system and related policies, and the effects of this cocktail of measurements that have been experienced so far.

THE COMMERCIAL SITUATION

Despite the fact that the ratification law was passed in 1998, the Malta Convention was only implemented in the legislation by the end of 2006. Since 1992, when the Convention was signed in Valletta, successive Ministers of Culture have been working on a proposal for a new Monuments Act. Nonetheless, for many years the major principles of the Malta Convention have already been put into practice as the ratification law created not so much legal, but *de facto* obligations for all levels of government. Therefore the soil disturbing activities of the national, regional or local governments already generate a lot of archaeological research. In addition, authorities have increasingly made 'preventive' archaeological research a condition

Figure 5.1 The Dutch archaeological discipline consists of one state service, four universities, nearly thirty municipality archaeologists and around twenty companies to carry out ca. 2000 (in 2006) mostly developer-funded archaeological projects (Photo Erfgoedinspectie).

for permits to private developers and sometimes even for citizens. As a result, substantial funding has been made available for archaeology. Estimates of the total volume of business amount to around 66 million Euro for 2004.

As these policy changes generated much more work, already in 2001 the free market system was introduced under a temporary decree to circumvent the legal restrictions of the current Monuments Act and companies were allowed to carry out archaeological fieldwork (figure 5.1) on the condition that they get permission from the State Archaeological Service (called the *Rijksdienst voor Archeologie, Cultuurlandschap en Monumenten*, RACM, as from September 2006). Legally, they cannot yet have a licence so they work by permission of the ROB and formally under the licence of the state service itself.

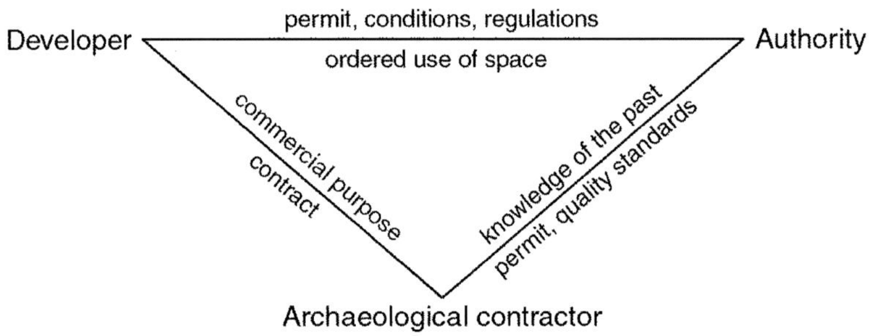

Figure 5.2 The organisation of the relation between the parties that are involved in the archaeological management, i.e. the authorities, the developer and the archaeological contractor and their (mutual) interests and relations.

By the end of 2005 there were nearly eighty private companies active on the archaeology market. Of these, 18 have permission to perform all kinds of excavation activities (including bore hole surveys) and 2 are allowed to perform bore hole surveys only. The others are doing various kinds of activities for which no licence is needed, such as surveys by field walking or remote sensing, consultancy, specialist services, presentations etc. After an explosive growth of new contractors between 2001 and 2004, the group of excavating companies has stabilised, but the group of non-licensed companies kept on growing. Especially consultancy is a growing business. Some of the excavating companies are quite large, with more than 50 and even up to 100 employees, but most of them are small with less than 10 staff members. In total, the archaeological community is estimated at around 1000 full time equivalents (fte) and the amount of registered field projects was hitherto growing each year, amounting to nearly 1800 in 2005.

THE QUALITY ASSURANCE APPROACH

Once the decision was taken that no longer only municipal archaeologists, universities and the state service were allowed to carry out excavations, the need for a quality assurance system became apparent that would clarify the responsibilities of the various parties (figure 5.2) that are involved in the archaeological heritage management process.

In the Dutch view, a just treatment of the archaeological resource and the acquisition of knowledge about the past is a government's responsibility and cannot be guaranteed by the mechanisms and instruments on the left part of the triangle, where both the developer and the archaeological contractor have important commercial concerns. There is too big a risk that commercial and financial interests

The ingredients of the Dutch quality assurance cocktail:

organised by legal means	**organised by self regulation**
– monuments act	– quality standard
– licence	– certificate
– inspectorate	– professional register
– central information system	– research agendas

Figure 5.3 In The Netherlands archaeological quality management is organised through a combination of legislative and private instruments.

will prevail. Therefore, the ministry set up a system in which the right side of the triangle remains responsible for the archaeological heritage. This means that the local, regional or national governments – dependent upon who is the responsible authority for the development concerned – decide on *what* must be investigated. They are responsible for the project outline on the basis of which a developer can put the project out for tender to archaeological contractors.

This construction does, however, not guarantee that the excavations, documentation and reports of the contractors meet the academic standards that are expected. Therefore, in addition to the construction of the responsibilities, a cocktail of quality assurance measurements was set up to make this construction work (figure 5.3).

This assemblage of instruments consists of a part that is organised through legislation and supervision, *and* a privately organised part which depends on self regulation. The idea was that the *strength* of the system would be found in the *coherence* of the system, with strong horizontal interactions between the separate elements on both sides and vertical interactions between the elements at each side.

The publicly organised part consists of a law, the just revised Monuments Act of 1988 (see for an English translation of the 1988 law the appendix to Willems 1997). In short, it states that nobody is allowed to excavate without a licence. Excavation is defined as 'moving the soil with the purpose to discover archaeological remains', and since November 2005 this also includes borehole surveys. This law has been revised in order to allow for commercial parties to carry out archaeological field projects. And according to this new law a permit is only given to those contractors that can demonstrate that they are capable of working according to the quality standard. So *here* there is a direct connection between the measurements at the right and the left side of figure 5.3. The revised law was submitted to Parliament in late 2005, and was accepted by Parliament in December, 2006. Details of what is discussed below may yet change as a result of the way in which decrees under the new law shall be phrased.

Another means to keep tight lines between the publicly and the privately organised instruments was established through an independent supervising organisation. At the time that the quality system was being designed, from 1999 onwards, it was decided that if a large part of the quality assurance system is delegated to the private sector, there should also be a mechanism to verify whether in practice the work is being done properly. For this purpose, a State Inspectorate for Archaeology was created in 2001 (which merged in with three other small cultural heritage inspectorates into the *Erfgoedinspectie* or State Inspectorate for Cultural Heritage at the beginning of 2006).

The main tasks of the inspectorate are to monitor compliance with the Monuments Act, to investigate the quality of the archaeological fieldwork and the resulting products, to monitor the functioning of the archaeological system as a whole and to inform the Minister of Culture on these aspects and related issues.

Last but not least, the public part includes a central information system maintained by the state service and developed out of the former sites and monuments register. It includes information on all sites and finds in the Netherlands and there is a legal obligation to report all information resulting from fieldwork and other activities (the Netherlands belongs to those countries which allow commercial archaeology but at the same time require all reports to be submitted. This precludes the possibility for developers or other patrons of archaeological companies to withhold information as is possible in some other countries, notably those with Anglo-Saxon legal systems).

As is usual in most of continental Europe, there is also a legal obligation to report chance finds.

The privately organised part of the system covers three levels:

- the level of the processes and procedures that concern the work in the field. For this a quality standard was developed that says *how* the archaeological processes should be carried out;
- the second level is that of the people and organisations. For this a professional register and a certification system were developed that say *who* are allowed to carry out particular activities, *i.e.* which companies and which employees meet the necessary demands;
- and finally for the level of the product, a research agenda was set up that will help the authorities to decide on *what* should be done, especially on the choices that they make regarding the research topics.

THE QUALITY STANDARD

At the privately organised part of the quality assurance system – on the right side of figure 5.3 – the key element is the quality standard. This was initiated by the Ministry of Culture, but it was developed by the archaeological community because it is believed that in order to successfully develop a standard, all relevant expertise must be involved and at the same time the commitment of the entire discipline is needed in order to successfully implement it in daily practice. Therefore a national preparatory committee was established in 1999, in which all parts of the discipline were represented: the universities, private companies, archaeological services of the local, regional and the national governments, the professional organisation Dutch Association of Archaeologists (NVvA) and also developers. Furthermore, an intensive process of consultation had to assure that the archaeological community was involved. Altogether, it took two years to develop and the Dutch Archaeology Quality Standard is now successfully operational since 2001 (in 2004 an English version of the standard was published by Willems and Brandt, it is also available as a pdf-file at www.erfgoedinspectie.nl/archeologie).

The standard covers six main processes of what is called the archaeological heritage management cycle; field evaluations, physical protection, excavations, watching briefs, depositing and registration. The process of selection was not included because that is essentially a decision that is taken by or on behalf of a government; it is not a commercial activity but a political decision on what is to happen, based on the outcome of the evaluation. There is no standard for interpretation and synthesis either. Obviously, standards have been developed for the initial analysis and interpretation in a report, which has to be produced within two years after the fieldwork has finished, but it was felt that further interpretation and synthetic work is scientific research that should not be regulated in the same way.

As it was acknowledged by the preparatory committee that much archaeological work is quite difficult to standardise and should not be made inflexible by too many prescriptions, the standard does not define all activities in detail but merely describes the requirements for each step in the process and for the documents that are involved, such as field drawings, distribution maps etc. Furthermore, the standard prescribes what kind of actor is allowed to carry out a particular activity (figure 5.4).

Another fundamental aspect of the quality control through the standard is that all critical steps must be checked, registered, and if necessary improved, by an actor with a particular status.

THE PROFESSIONAL REGISTER

As the standard puts a lot of responsibility in the hands of the individual actors, and distinguishes conditional operations which are reserved for archaeologists with a particular expertise, this also introduced the need to define the required capabilities of the actors and, subsequently, an assessment of those archaeologists that want to carry out these conditional operations. Therefore, also in 1999, the Dutch Association of Archaeologists (*Nederlandse Vereniging van Archeologen*, NVvA) was asked and facilitated by the Ministry of Culture to develop a national 'register of archaeologists' that would contain the names of the archaeologists which are allowed to take care of the reserved activities.

Figure 5.4 In the quality standard it is prescribed what kind of actor is allowed to carry out a particular (crucial) activity, both in the field and during the analysis (Photo Erfgoedinspectie).

The initial idea was that there would be a direct connection between the key actors in the standard and in the professional register and that all archaeologists would be registered according to education, training and experience into three categories. For a number of reasons, this approach was eventually not followed

Figure 5.5 The lack of an operational professional register implies that there is not yet an assessment of most of the 'key persons' that the quality standard distinguishes (Photo Erfgoedinspectie).

by the association and they designed a register that consists of two categories (Perk 2004). The higher category of registered archaeologist involves a peer review system for admission, and the system is includes an obligation for CPD, continuing professional development (see Aitchison 2006 for a discussion of what this may entail).

The proposals were accepted by the members of the association in December 2004, but unfortunately, when this paper was written (early 2006) the proposals had not been put into practice and the professional register was not yet operational. One of the main reasons for this is that the proposed approach, especially the peer review system does not seem to meet the demands of objectivity that certification rules require.

The obvious consequence of a non-operational register is that the quality assurance cocktail lacks a very important ingredient. It implies that there is not yet an assessment of most of the key figures that the quality standard distinguishes while meanwhile the contractors already carry out these activities (figure 5.5). This is a major risk for the quality system. Since 2001, the State Inspectorate has encountered several situations in which inexperienced or even incompetent archaeologists were carrying out conditional and reserved operations and subsequently performed poorly. Another implication of not having a professional register is that there is no opportunity to 'punish' individuals by removing them from the register in case of severe un-ethic behaviour. This, however, is provisionally covered by the requirement in the quality standard that archaeologists working in heritage management must subscribe to a code of ethics, which can be demonstrated by membership in a professional organisation with a grievance committee: not just the Dutch one (NVvA), but also the English Institute for Field Archaeologists (see Hinton and Jennings, this volume) or the American Register of Professional Archaeologists (see Peacock and Rafferty, this volume) are acceptable.

THE CERTIFICATION SYSTEM

During the years that the register was under construction, a certification system for archaeological companies has been designed as well. The new Monuments Act requires a licence to excavate and of course the system must provide for a method to guarantee that organisations – both governmental excavation services and private companies – that want to obtain a licence are evaluated with respect to their ability to work according to the Standard. At the moment, it has not been decided yet if this shall be done by certification, whereby organisations are audited and must obtain a certificate on the basis of which a licence is given, or if it will be done by the government.

The original idea was that a certificate would be granted by independent certification agencies and would verify – on the basis of assessments and audits – if companies or institutes have the right equipment, the necessary internal procedures, qualified personnel etc. at their disposal and that can make it plausible that they are able and willing to live up to the quality standards. The Ministry could then recognise such a private certificate and issue licences upon request to certified parties. In the Netherlands, this is currently the preferred approach in many other fields where the government wants control but does not want to organise the quality control itself.

Although the archaeological community was not against such a system, and indeed developed the criteria for certification, commercial parties were only prepared to actually go ahead with this if the Ministry would make the certificate a legal obligation with no 'back doors'. This, however, did not happen as apparently it would be against policies of deregulation. This has led to a kind of stalemate and implies that either the certificate will only be used as an instrument by which contractors voluntarily can distinguish themselves from others, that it is replaced by an equivalent system, or that it will not be implemented at all. The chances of voluntary certification are slim, however, because substantial costs are involved for contractors. In that case, the ministry still has to come up with a decree concerning the procedure of admittance before the new Monuments Act is accepted by the parliament. This may well take the form of an evaluation procedure that is more or less equivalent to certification, but organised entirely within the civil service (State Service and/or Inspectorate). Fortunately, during the parliamentary discussion of the revised law, it became clear that whatever road is taken, the Quality Standard is fully accepted as the basis for evaluation of suitability of licence holders.

THE NATIONAL RESEARCH AGENDA

A final element that was considered important for the Dutch quality assurance system is that relevant research objectives for archaeological field research are pointed out. The quality standard only provides the framework, as it requires that any field project is based on a project outline or brief that contains the research questions; it specifies *what* must be investigated, and *how*. This still is no guarantee, however, that academically relevant and useful questions are being asked. In the past, national research goals were set by the State Service and by the universities, and local goals by the towns with a municipal archaeologist. Now, due to decentralization of government, decisions for most fieldwork lie in the hands of local authorities (ca. 450 municipalities) that do not have their own archaeologist. Therefore, the need for 'research agendas' was perceived, preferably both at the national and at regional levels, that can provide guidance for these local authorities. The work on a research agenda at the national level started in 2004, and again representatives of all branches within the discipline were involved in what turned out to be a huge endeavour. Altogether more than seventy people were involved and together they wrote a 'research bible' of more than 800 pages. Fortunately it was published on a website that recently became operational (www.noaa.nl).

The aim is to link the quality standard statutorily with the research agenda in order to make sure that the aims on the agenda are taken into account in project outlines for excavations and field evaluations.

FIRST EXPERIENCES

The above outline describes the development of a Dutch perspective on an archaeological quality assurance system and how this is influenced by policy changes, legal barriers and opportunities, and other considerations. All this, however, is still only the theory. Logically, the next issue is to explore whether it works in practice. At this moment, this cannot yet be answered fairly. Not only have major and crucial parts of the system not yet been fully implemented or perhaps may never become operational, but also the legal framework within which the system is meant to function, will only become operational in 2007. This means that, for example, funding was not always available.

Notwithstanding the fact that our quality assurance system is not fully operational and that the coherence of the system is still far from optimal, there are certainly some positive effects. It can be seen, for instance, that nearly all archaeologists comply with the standard and that most of the work in the field meets its demands.

The effect of this is that the quality of data and documentation is more comparable and coherent and therefore more durable and better accessible for future analytical research. Furthermore, results of field projects are in the majority of cases being published within two years. This is a huge improvement in comparison with the traditional situation, in which the majority of the excavations never were published. Its importance cannot be overstated, as the enormous and growing backlog of half a century of unpublished or just superficially published excavations is a major problem for archaeological heritage management all around the world (for example, Hadjisavvas and Karageorghis 2000). Another improvement of great importance is that all information on sites and projects is reported and put into the central archaeological information system. The implication is, that not only the backlog of unpublished excavations is no longer growing each year, also the enormous problem of an ever increasing volume of grey literature has been halted (see *e.g.* Hills 1993; Lauwerier and De Vries 2002).

The benefit for future research will be enormous. Even if it is recognised that the fact that all reports are now accessible this is of course no guarantee for their quality, at least the data are available. Moreover, the actual quality of reports is also monitored and it is expected to gradually improve. This may already be going on, though for the moment it cannot yet be demonstrated. What *can* be demonstrated, however, is that with the rising volume of total output and despite shortcomings to be discussed below, there is a clear rise in the number of high quality reports that is beginning to exert an influence on Dutch archaeological research.

A final positive effect is that the development of the individual parts of the quality system generated the unique experience of a whole archaeological community that is intensively and successfully working together. Without creating a false impression of a totally harmonious community of Dutch archaeologists it can still be said that by this process divides have been bridged and cooperative ties have been strengthened across the discipline.

Nonetheless, there are also aspects that need serious attention. While most of the procedural demands are met during the work in the field, there seems to be less attention for the scientific demands. Three recent studies have shown that especially the quality of the knowledge products, such as project outlines, site evaluations and final reports is far from sufficiently guaranteed.

For instance in an orientation study that the State Inspectorate carried out in 2003 on the quality of 15 project outlines for field evaluation projects, it was found that they contained only thirty percent of the requirements concerning content (Aten *et al.* 2003). For example, only one of the five project outlines for 'surveys' provided research questions, and also only one project outline gave a justification for the prescribed research method. Fortunately the project outlines for excavations were considerably better as they contained on average half of the requirements, but the overall picture was not very satisfactory.

At that time it was presumed that the archaeological community needed some time to get acquainted with the quality standard, with writing good project outlines and with the commercial way of working. Therefore, the inspectorate waited until 2004 to start a study on the quality of the reports on field evaluations. For this study (Aten *et al.* 2005), the latest published report was selected of each of the 20 companies that were performing field evaluations at that time, of three municipal archaeologists and of the State Service.

This time it was found that in most reports much of the required basic information is present, but that there is still far less academic content, let alone *relevant* content. For instance, only in one third of the reports specific research questions were mentioned that related to the expected archaeological phenomena. The aim of the other projects merely was to trace and to date find spots. Furthermore, in only two reports a motivation was given for the research strategy that was chosen. It seems that in the other projects a standard procedure had been applied without a validation of the reliability or the applicability of the method in relation to what archaeological phenomena were to be expected.

A third study that was published in 2005 by the state archaeological service. It involved 100 project outlines and 39 reports (Bazelmans *et al.* 2005). Unfortunately this study was biased as it only involved the products of 13 companies and none of universities or municipalities, but again, the conclusion was that the scientific quality is disappointing. More than half (52%) of the project outlines was judged to be unsatisfactory and one fourth was even considered totally unacceptable. The excavation reports were found to be slightly better than the project outlines, as 56% was found to be satisfactory. Nonetheless, the average appreciation of the quality of the reports was quite lean (5.5) as well and again there was a fairly high percentage (19%) of very bad reports.

Apart from these studies that clearly demonstrate the deficiencies, there are also less firm indications that the quality of the archaeological work is not sufficiently assured yet. There are, for example, signals from within the archaeological community itself that people are worried about the academic quality of the Malta-projects. Despite the fact that the archaeological community has put a lot of effort in developing a quality system, with the intention to guarantee a certain academic level of the output, there seems to be a growing tendency to perform field projects merely as a craft rather than a scientific enterprise. In proportion to the enormous growth of jobs and projects in the last say ten years – respectively around 400% (from 250 to 1000 fte) and 600% (from 300 to 1750) – there is not as much profit in terms of scientific output. In other words, although in absolute terms the annual number of high quality reports is certainly rising that is not yet so in relative terms and it may be concluded that the return on investment or value for money in terms of academic output and relevant research results is not as high as the investment itself. In the long term this may become a serious problem, because already regional authorities start using it as an argument to cut down the financing of archaeological research.

THE NEED FOR ADDITIONAL MEASURES

The archaeological community as a whole is aware of the shortcomings. And in an attempt to improve the quality of the output, various parties have initiated a whole range of remedies. Some of these measures have not left the drawing table yet, such as a plea for more state interference and financial support to facilitate granting of projects with outstanding academic prospects to university departments. Others, however, are already put into practice. For instance, work is now being done on developing supplementary guidelines or 'best practices' for excavations and all companies must now use a standard model to write project outlines, so important elements cannot be left out. Some local authorities have set up their own guidelines for particular practices, such as scenarios for field surveys with prescriptions relating to the grid and density of trial trenches or boreholes in certain geological situations. The organisation that administers the quality standard has investigated the needs and possibilities for (re)training programs.

It is of course very important that the archaeological community signals the problem and is willing to work on improvements, and some of these truly are important initiatives that may indeed be helpful. However, they hardly influence the more fundamental issues that are causing the difficulties that we are faced with.

The main problem is that at the moment the system has insufficient incentives to encourage the production of a relevant research output. The results of the various studies on the quality of the output, together with the audits of the inspectorate at field projects, show that much of the commercial archaeological fieldwork is degrading towards a craft rather than a scientific enterprise. The reasons for this are clear. First of all, the contractors that are engaged in archaeological work have to deal with a ferocious economic competition: there are not enough profitable projects and contractors fight each other for work. As a result, they have to drop their prices and the profit margin is declining below what is economically sustainable. This is not something that the contractors can be blamed for, this is how the commercial world works. However, the undesirable side effect is that it leads to a situation in which there often is hardly enough money and time to put a real effort in the knowledge products such as excavation reports. Added to a shortage of qualified and experienced employees who are capable to perform on an academic level while the time constraints are getting worse, this will eventually lead to a loss of quality of the output.

Second, most developers, builders etc. are hardly interested in the end product in terms of scientific results, yet they select which contractor is going to do the job. This encourages that their choice is primarily based on economic grounds and on a contractor's abilities to master the project, but not on the contractor's academic qualities.

Third, within the development-led archaeology we are not very much focussed on getting the most out of the field projects in terms of knowledge gain. We lack, for instance, a lively discourse within the archaeological community in relation to the development-led archaeology. Companies, municipalities and universities are largely working on their own, there is not much dialogue going on with regard to the results of the field projects in archaeological terms. In addition, and as a result of being a small country, we do not have a flourishing academic journal and there are relatively few conferences on academic subjects. Therefore there is not a lot of stimulation from colleagues, neither by means of appreciation or reward for good practices nor by means of 'punishment' for bad practices (see also Van den Dries 2005 for an analysis of the knowledge management activities and opportunities of the Dutch archaeological discipline). Formerly, when the archaeological community was still small, much of this was compensated for by a very international orientation that was practically unavoidable in the past because of the smallness of the language community. As has been shown recently by Kristiansen (2001), the growth of the discipline in smaller language communities in Europe, has demonstrably led to a loss in international orientation.

Unfortunately there are no simple solutions for these fundamental issues. We are dealing with a complex situation with – on the one hand – competing economic and academic concerns and – on the other hand – a government that wants deregulation instead of an increased interference by the authorities. To a certain point, it may help if the functioning of the quality control system will be optimised according to the way it was set up, but this will not 'make' people think in a scientific way and it cannot force them to keep up with the state of the academic art and to contribute to the research progress as long as the right climate is missing. If the archaeological community seriously wants to do something about it, it must start to acknowledge that the direction we are heading for is not the direction that we had in mind when we started.

CONCLUSION: LESSONS LEARNED

Returning to the issue of quality assurance, the process of change did teach some important lessons and although the situation differs in each country, these lessons may certainly be relevant elsewhere. A first lesson is that the cocktail of measurements seems to be a useful approach, as long as all of them operate in the way they were originally intended to. If even one of them is missing, the system immediately looses its balance and things go wrong. Furthermore, we have experienced that if the quality assurance system has to be built up from scratch, as it had to be in our case, it is important to get commitment from the entire archaeological community. This can for instance be accomplished by encouraging representatives of all fields (consultants, academics, municipal archaeologists, state archaeologists etc.) to be involved and to take care of particular parts of the quality system, such as the quality standard, research agendas and the professional register.

Figure 5.6 The Dutch quality assurance system was established by applying the 'poldermodel': the interests of all parties were considered (Photo Gerlo Beernink Fotografie).

For many, this may seem the ultimate example of the famous Dutch 'poldermodel' (figure 5.6), which means that all parties must be involved in the decision making in order to reach a decision that is acceptable by all parties, but which also implies that in many cases the decision is considered to be a feeble, tasteless or 'flat' compromise. In our case it would not have worked otherwise. Since we endeavoured a rather drastic change in the archaeological heritage management system, the only way was to take the interest of all parties into account. With such a large group of persons involved, it surely takes quite a while to establish consensus, but the result is that almost the entire community approves the results. This does not mean that the entire community is pleased with the situation of commercial archaeology as a whole, but given the way that policymakers have dictated the way to implement the Malta Convention, the general attitude towards the quality assurance system is one of acceptance.

A final lesson, however, is that a quality assurance system is not enough to guarantee the quality of the end product, *i.e.* the knowledge that is gained by the archaeological work. Therefore quality assurance should be combined with knowledge management to obtain a more complete quality management approach.

References

Aitchison, K. (2006) You say PCE, I say CPD. Training for professional archaeologists in the UK. *SAA Archaeological Record* 6 (2), 20–22.

Aten, N. A., M. H. van den Dries, G. R. M. van den Eynde and D. H. de Jager (2003) *Een Goed begin. Een verkennend onderzoek naar het gebruik van de Kwaliteitsnorm Nederlandse Archeologie bij het opstellen van Programma's van Eisen.* (RIA-Rapport 1). Den Haag.

Aten, N. A., M. H. van den Dries, G. R. M. van den Eynde, D. H. de Jager and S. Boogert (2005) *IVO op niveau? Een onderzoek naar de kwaliteit van rapporten van archeologisch inventariserend veldonderzoek.* (RIA-Rapport 2) Den Haag.

Bazelmans, J. G. A., O. Brinkkemper, J. H. C. Deeben, J. van Doesburg, R. C. G. M. Lauwerier and P. A. M. Zoetbrood (2005) *Mag het ietsje meer zijn? Een onderzoek naar door bedrijven opgestelde Programma's van Eisen voor archeologisch onderzoek uit de periode 2003–2004.* (Rapportage Archeologische Monumentenzorg 120). Amersfoort.

Dries, M. H. van den (2005) Kennismanagement: de missing link voor Malta? In M. H. van den Dries and W. J. H. Willems (eds) *Innovatie in de Nederlandse Archeologie*, 161–177. Gouda.

Hadjisavvas, S. and V. Karageorghis (eds) (2000) *The problem of unpublished excavations.* Nicosia.

Hills, C. (1993) The dissemination of information. In J. Hunter and I. Ralston (eds) *Archaeological Resource Management in the UK. An Introduction*, 215–224. Phoenix Mill.

Kristiansen, K. (2001) Borders of ignorance: research communities and language. In Z. Kobyliński (ed.) *Quo vadis archaeologia? Whither European archaeology in the 21st century*, 38–43. Warsaw.

Lauwerier, R. C. G. M. and L. S. de Vries (2002) Lifting the Iceberg – BoneInfo and the Battle to Save Archaeological Information. In R. C. G. M. Lauwerier and I. Plug (eds) *The Future from the Past*, 167–175. Oxford.

Perk, F. A. (ed.) (2004) *Het beroepsregister voor archeologen. Een blauwdruk.* Amsterdam.

Willems, W. J. H. (1997) Archaeological Heritage Management in the Netherlands: past, present and future. In W. J. H. Willems, H. Kars and D. P. Hallewas (eds) *Archaeological Heritage Management in the Netherlands*, 3–34. Amersfoort/Assen.

Willems, W. J. H. (2005) Contract Archaeology and Quality Management in the Netherlands. In M. H. van den Dries and W. J. H. Willems (eds) *Innovatie in de Nederlandse Archeologie*, 153–161. Gouda.

Willems, W. J. H. and R. W. Brandt (eds) (2004) *Dutch Archaeology Quality Standard.* (RIA-report). Den Haag.

CHAPTER 6

Quality management in Romanian archaeology

Mircea Angelescu

INTRODUCTION

The integrated management of the cultural heritage and the integrated and sustainable social and economic development of communities are the main objectives of the development of the legal framework of Romanian archaeology. Compliance with the underlying concepts both of the relevant European conventions such as the Granada and Valletta Conventions, Berne and Florence Conventions, as well as the new Framework Convention on the Value of Cultural Heritage for the Society – Faro Convention (Council of Europe 1985, 1992, 2000, 2005; World Intellectual Property Organization 1886) and of the working methods advocated in the reference texts on sustainable development such as the Hannover Principles of McDonough and Braungart (1992; available on the internet at http://www.mcdonough.com/principles.pdf) or the Pan-European Biological and Landscape Diversity Strategy (see http://www.strategyguide.org) has been a matter of concern since 2000. Archaeology is one of the pillars of the heritage policies (strategies and action programs) of the Ministry of Culture. In practice, protection of the archaeological heritage is ensured by the provisions of the Law no. 182/2000 (revised) on the protection of the movable heritage, the Law no. 422/2001 (revised) on the protection of historical monuments and Government Ordnance no. 43/2000. These three texts together constitute the legal framework for protection of the cultural heritage in Romania.

THE LEGAL FRAMEWORK

The first law on the protection of the archaeological heritage was Government Ordinance no. 43/2000. It radically transformed Romanian archaeology by defining for the first time the different types of archaeological research, the different types of legal protection, chance finds, the Register of Archaeologists, the role of the National Committee for Archaeology, the legal obligation to report all information to a central information system that is maintained by the Ministry of Culture, the conditions required for obtaining the archaeological excavation permits, as well as the various competencies of the central and local administrations. It also introduced articles that marked the real entry into force of the 'polluter pays' principle and, last but not least, it established penalties for different offences affecting the archaeological heritage.

The Romanian law on the archaeological heritage is defining and protecting:

- archaeological research (Government Ordinance no. 43/2000 (revised) art. 2 reads: 'archaeological research is understood to be an ensemble of scientific and technical measures meant to ensure prospecting, identification, uncovering by archaeological excavations, investigation, collection, registration and scientific assessing of archaeological heritage, including publication; archaeological research is being carried out in terms of the present ordnance by specialized staff certified and registered in the Register of Archaeologists. The results of archaeological research are based on the legal system for protecting archaeological discoveries or, as suitable, of releasing archaeological charge of the respective area');
- archaeological discovery;
- archaeological discovery made by chance (fortuitous archaeological discovery);
- areas with known and researched archaeological heritage;
- archaeological sites declared as areas of national interest;
- areas with located archaeological heritage;
- areas with archaeological potential uncovered by chance.

Although there have already been two updates of this first legal framework (Laws 378/2001 and 462/2003), these did not affect the system established by Government Ordinance no. 43/2000. The modifications were part of the continuous effort to adapt the law to the challenges that arose after introducing the new legal framework. A new modification that will enter into force by July 2006 introduces some articles regarding archaeological standards as well as provisions for the European Landscape Convention, in an effort to achieve an integrated heritage protection system and to establish administrative mechanisms for the protection, management and planning of Romanian territory that will eventually lead to the establishment of a landscape policy.

QUALITY CONTROL

Even more recently, in 2004, Romanian archaeology also adopted a system of quality control in the field of archaeology. The fact that a self-regulating system of this profession did not exist led the Archaeological Department of the Ministry of Culture to build such a system, in accordance with the European Convention on the protection of the archaeological heritage of Valletta (Council of Europe 1992). This was ratified by Romania by Law no. 150 of the 24th of July 1997 that affirms in its preamble: '... it is important to institute, where they do not yet exist, appropriate administrative and scientific supervision procedures ...'.

It is often asserted that in Romanian archaeology today, the quality of archaeological work is diminishing continually. But such assertions remain unsubstantiated: no one

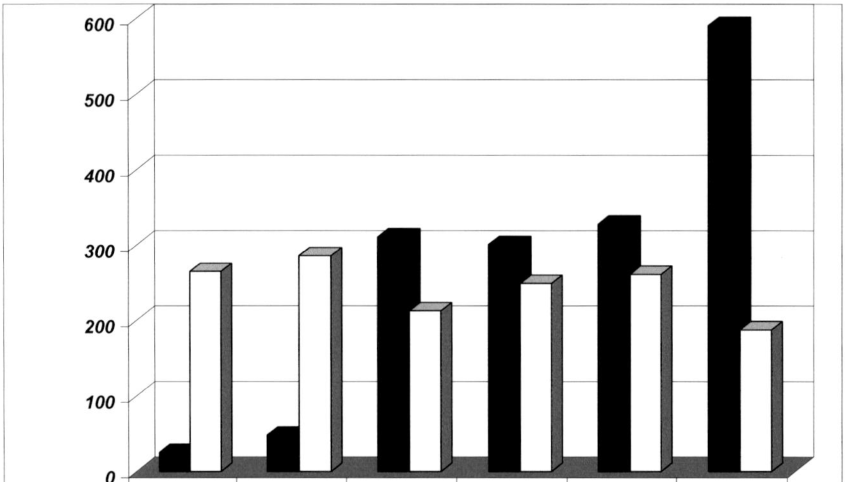

	2000	2001	2002	2003	2004	2005
■ Preventive	25	48	311	301	328	591
□ Systematic	265	286	213	249	261	188

Figure 6.1 The preventive versus the systematic archaeological investigations in Romania.

can say exactly what this would consist of. Usually we have to wait for many years before an excavation is finally published – if indeed this ever happens! – to be able to determine if an archaeologist did his job in a proper way.

The pressure of the continuously growing number of preventive against systematic archaeological investigations (see figure 6.1) has made it clear that there is a need to establish quality standards to ensure the protection and the preservation of the archaeological heritage. This heritage faces large scale investment projects all over the country that raise new methodological and technical problems with important administrative and juridical consequences. Preventive archaeology is defined (in Government Ordinance no. 43/2000 (revised), art. 2) as: "archaeological researches caused by works of construction, modification, enlargement or repairs of means of communication, technical-utility endowment, including underground or underwater, excavations, exploitation of spots for supplying materials, construction of main pipe line networks, arrangements for land improvement, means of telecommunications, erecting relays and telecommunication aerials, works for researching and prospecting grounds – drillings or excavations – necessary to do geotechnical studies, to find locations for gravel extraction and wells for gas and oil, as well as other works that affect the soil surface in areas with located archaeological heritage, within as well as outside of built-up areas and irrespective of the form of property upon that land". Systematic research is defined in the same article as:

"archaeological researches performed on a large scale and during several years, executed according to a research project".

The realities of development needs in present day modern society have made it clear that we need an objective approach to research, a model that allows us to accurately register and to compare between different and various archaeological projects that are to be carried out and to ascertain a maximum quantity and quality of data and information about the past. On the other hand, the Valletta Convention states that the competent authority (*i.e.* the Government) should not give a permit to a developer if valuable archaeological remains are endangered. However, if economic, social and other interests are considered to be more important, archaeological research must be done according to standards that are endorsed by the national competent authority – a warrant for the quality of the necessary archaeological work.

The quality management system of Romanian archaeology is organized into two levels: the first level concerns quality assurance of the process or methodology (standards, procedures, methods, code of conduct, best practice guides etc.), the second level concerns the quality of the product: the content and relevance of the scientific results (national and regional strategies; local, regional and national research agendas, etc.).

THE FIRST LEVEL: QUALITY ASSURANCE OF THE PROCESS

The basic level has three main directions that are followed systematically for the management of the quality of archaeological work: the Romanian Register of Archaeologists; archaeological quality standards and a code of conduct for archaeologists.

The Romanian Register of Archaeologists

The legal basis for the existence of the Register is an article in the Governmental Ordinance no. 43 (revised) that reads: "Archaeological research is performed according to this Ordinance, by the specialised staff certified and registered in the Register of Archaeologists." No archaeological research that involves excavation can be done legally by anyone without being registered. Moreover, all excavations, watching briefs or archaeological assessments are subject to a mandatory permit issued by the Ministry of Culture.

Registered archaeologists are placed into three levels, based on academic and experience criteria (see figure 6.2). Archaeological experience is quantified by points awarded for each time-unit of 2 weeks field research during the studies or after graduation from the University.

The main result of this system is that a minimum academic quality of archaeological work is guaranteed by the different levels of university training and on the other hand the importance of practical field experience is valued.

Debutant	University studies + MA degree	At least 2 months of archaeological experience	Can be part of an archaeological research team
Specialist	University studies + MA degree + PhD in course + a minimum of 7 studies published	At least 8 months of archaeological experience	Can be responsible for part of a systematic or preventive intervention. In special cases, can manage a preventive intervention
Expert	PhD + minimum of 15 studies published + 1 book	At least 12 months of archaeological experience	Can be responsible for a systematic or a preventive intervention

Figure 6.2 The levels of the Register of Archaeologists.

ARCHAEOLOGICAL QUALITY STANDARDS

Before the appearance of Government Ordinance no. 43, there was no legal basis in Romania for deciding on the quality of the archaeological research that was being carried out. After some modifications of this Ordinance (Laws no. 378/2001 and 462/2003), the Ministry of Culture and Religious Affairs issued the Order no. 2392/2004 in September 2004. The standards and procedures adopted by this Order were largely inspired by those of the British Institute of Field Archaeologists (see Hinton and Jennings, this volume). A new and different edition of the standard was issued in March 2005 (Angelescu 2005).

Starting with the new modification of the law the system of quality standards will be based on the law. The reason is that in this way the system will have much more juridical weight. But it must be mentioned that, for reasons of an obvious need for flexibility, the contents of the standard will still remain to be established by a ministry order.

The important investments in infrastructure projects in recent years produced a series of big archaeological projects. Practice has shown that such large scale research projects require a major effort to achieve in practice the levels of cross-disciplinary cooperation that are needed. There emerged a need for a clearer structure of the objectives and a coherent methodological approach. Besides that, all these projects brought forward the importance of data management and of creating rigorous and precise site archives that will preserve the information gathered by different means for future research and interpretation. These circumstances imposed a sudden and strong development of field inventories and of mapping systems that suddenly were discovered as the main method to collect, interpret and utilize data about historical monuments and archaeological sites and as a source of information to rely on. Well structured archives, with consistent and high quality archaeological data that comply with international standards are one of the main objectives of the standards and procedures.

The standards are not intended to provide mandatory rules to be applied during

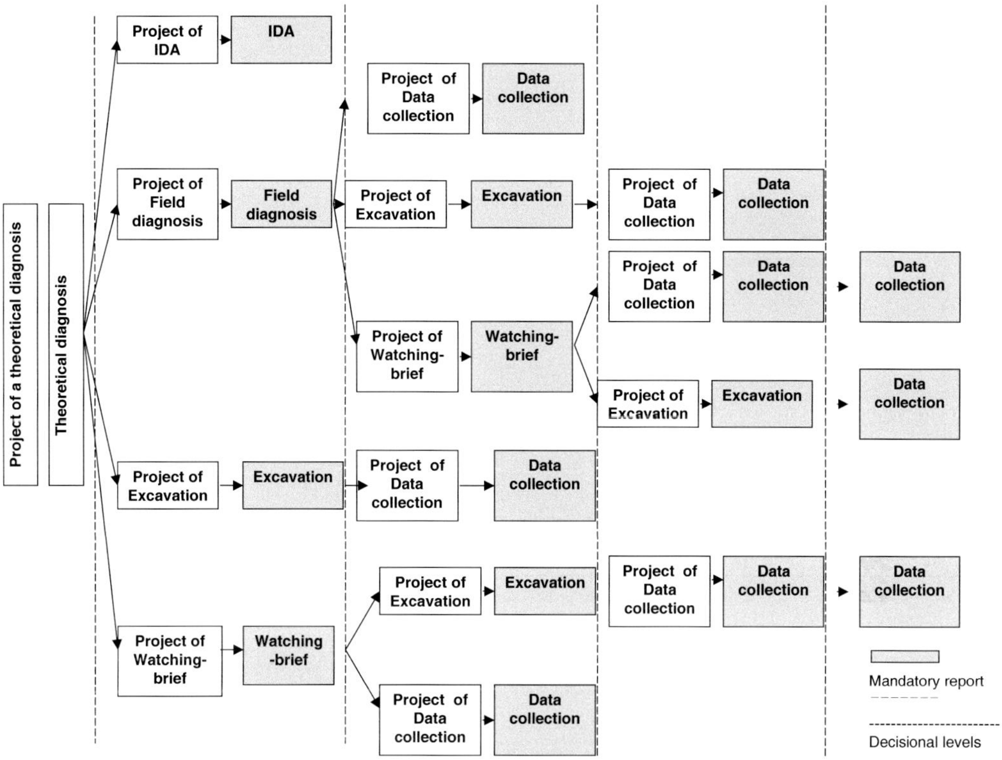

Figure 6.3 The stages of the archaeological process (theoretical or field diagnosis, excavation, watching-brief, archaeological data collection) that must be started by a specific project design and ended by a report, according to the quality standard.

the research process. First of all, they state that all stages of the archaeological process (theoretical or field diagnosis, excavation, watching-brief, archaeological data collection) must begin by a specific project design and must end by writing a report (see figure 6.3).

There are definitions for the diagnosis (with two sub-types: documentary and field diagnosis), archaeological excavation, watching-brief, collection of archaeological material, recording of archaeological data and processing of the material. Every definition is completed by a general objective and by a set of specific objectives that have to be met in order to ensure compliance with the standard.

Each standard describes the minimum of research work that must be done in order to ensure that a specific archaeological activity will produce enough data to allow a proper interpretation of the excavation and/or site(s). The procedures define best practices for carrying out archaeological projects and for the public communication of the results (see figure 6.4).

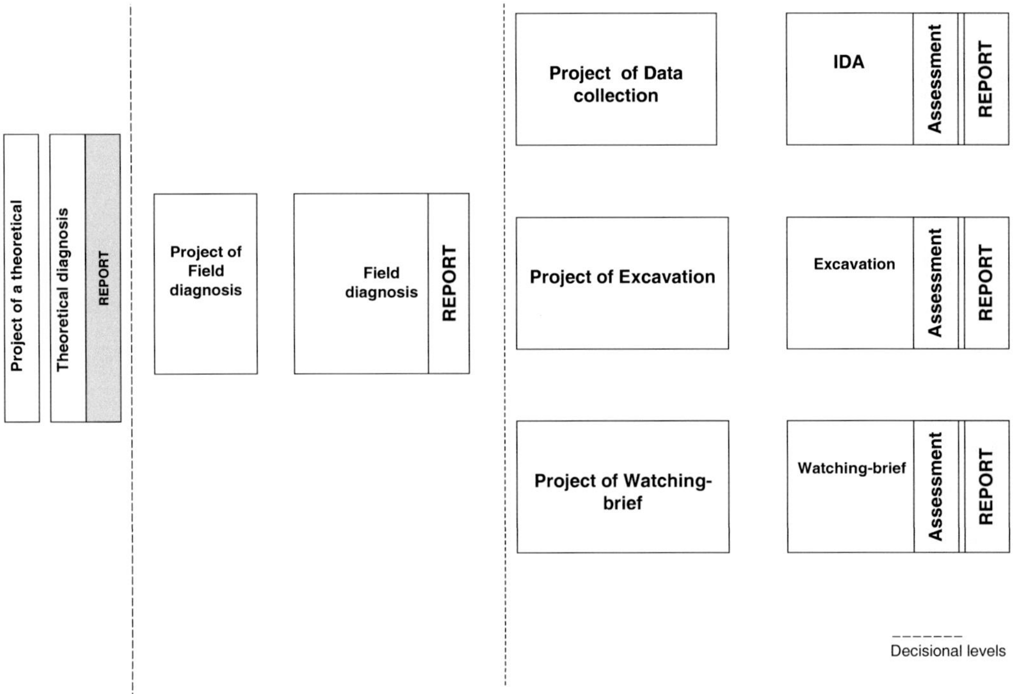

Figure 6.4 Each standard describes the minimum of research work that must be done in order to allow a proper interpretation.

The main idea is that archaeology is first of all academic research. Trying to systemize the different stages of this process, the enumeration of the techniques that are used in the field, the regulation of the methods that are best to be used for registering the results of the work and the public communication and dissemination of the results are the main objectives. The definitions, the standards and the procedures leave enough room for the archaeologist's initiatives and creativeness. These are not rules that are to be followed with a view to obtain final products that are identical or depersonalised – they are intended to be general norms that will help archaeologists valorise the results of their work based on the individual academic contribution.

On the other hand, due to the intensive development of the last years there is a continuously growing demand for preventive archaeological interventions. This type of work is introducing two constraints that the Romanian archaeologist was not familiar with until recently: time and money. There were two consequences: archaeology started to be seen by some as a service and a new type of relationship developed between archaeologists and contractors.

That is why it became obvious that only contract-led work could ensure the proper conditions for this type of work. It is only by such a contract that the investor has a guarantee of not paying too much for the work he needs to have done and of his time schedule being respected; conversely, the archaeologist obtains assurance that the technical and financial means needed for his work will become available. Under these conditions, archaeological research is done as a consequence of a contract between the investors and the archaeologists. It is a matter of crucial importance that archaeologists have at their disposal an instrument that will allow them to have enough time and resources to obtain the most relevant knowledge about the past (*i.e.* site/sites excavated).

The competent government authorities (the Ministry of Culture and its deconcentrated services), on the other hand, have at their disposal a set of rules that is intended to ensure that a minimum of the academic requirements and of archaeological quality are maintained in a system that is primarily based on the management of time and financial resources. Preservation or protection of the environment (including archaeology and natural heritage), protected structures and architectural conservation areas must be mandatory 'objectives' for archaeological research. The standards and the procedures cover exactly these rules.

Archaeological code of conduct

The Romanian Register of Archaeologists provides a set of rules determining *who* is permitted to conduct excavations. The archaeological standards and procedures are defining *how* the archaeological work should be done. The Code of Conduct is instituting a set of moral rules for the archaeologists.

The code is mainly based on the European Association of Archaeologist's (EAA) Code of Practice approved by the members of the association at the annual business meeting, held in Ravenna (Italy) in 1997 and on the EAA Principles of Conduct for archaeologists involved in contract archaeological work, approved by the members of the association at Göteborg (Sweden) in 1998. The Code states mainly that all archaeological work should be carried out in the spirit of the Charter for the management of the archaeological heritage approved by ICOMOS (International Council on Monuments and Sites) in 1990, that the archaeologists should take all the necessary measures to ensure the preservation of the archaeological heritage and, if preservation is impossible, they ensure that investigations are carried out to the highest professional standards concerning both the heritage and the environment. There are also provisions on the training, curation and publication and on avoiding all forms of discrimination.

As far as contract archaeology is concerned, the code has provisions on understanding of, and operating within, the legal framework, on avoiding all types of conflicts of interest and on ensuring that developers and planners are properly advised while they understand their responsibilities and relationships in the national structure. On the other hand, archaeologists involved in contract archaeological work will ensure the collection and preservation of all archaeological information and will be conscious of the need to maintain the academic coherence of their profession.

THE SECOND LEVEL: QUALITY OF THE PRODUCT

This level is concerned with the validation of archaeological projects and of archaeological reports in terms of the quality of the 'product'. Its main aim is to ensure that development-led archaeological research will always be relevant and make a contribution to our better knowledge of the uncovered material and structures, of the site(s) and, finally, to our understanding of the past.

By the provisions of the law on the protection of the archaeological heritage the content and relevance of academic results should be guaranteed by the existence of a coherent and consistent strategy. The main body responsible for defining the national research strategy is the National Archaeological Committee. The national strategy will ensure that academic research is set in a proper and indispensable framework and that the main directions of action are settled by action plans.

It is, however, also important to stress the importance of local, regional and national research agendas. Starting from the realities and the needs of each territorial unit, from the areas that are characterised by the same landscape features, we will obtain a general overview of the actual state of Romanian archaeology.

The National Committee for Archaeology is organised as a specialised scientific body, without being a legal person. It has an advisory role within the Ministry of Culture and Religions and is made up of specialists in the field, who are employed by archaeological institutes, museums, as well as by other institutions. They are responsible for developing strategies and they give qualified advice on national programs for research, methodologies, and on normative and technical-scientific regulations in the field of archaeological research. The members of this scientific committee are charged with reviewing requests for permits for archaeological excavations, irrespective of their source of financing. The committee establishes criteria and gives qualified advice on certification of specialists and experts in the field of archaeological research, included in the Register of Archaeologists. It also produces advice studies to underpin decisions to define, institute and delimit areas of protection that comprise archaeological heritage, it analyses the lawsuits in its field of competence, gives qualified advice on training programs for specialists and on plans for specialisation in the field of archaeological research.

As one can easily understand the National Committee for Archaeology is ensuring the academic basis for all the administrative decisions of the Ministry of Culture, in the field of archaeology (figure 6.5). On the basis of the expert advice of the committee, the competent authority (Ministry of Culture) will take the administrative action: to demand that a watching brief or an excavation is undertaken, to impose the conservation *in situ* of a part or the totally of the discoveries or to issue an Archaeological Discharge Certificate (that is cancelling all legal protection that previously existed).

The interaction between the two levels of the Romanian archaeological quality management system results in a mechanism that strives to achieve the quality in the result of the work of the professionals at all stages: from the project design

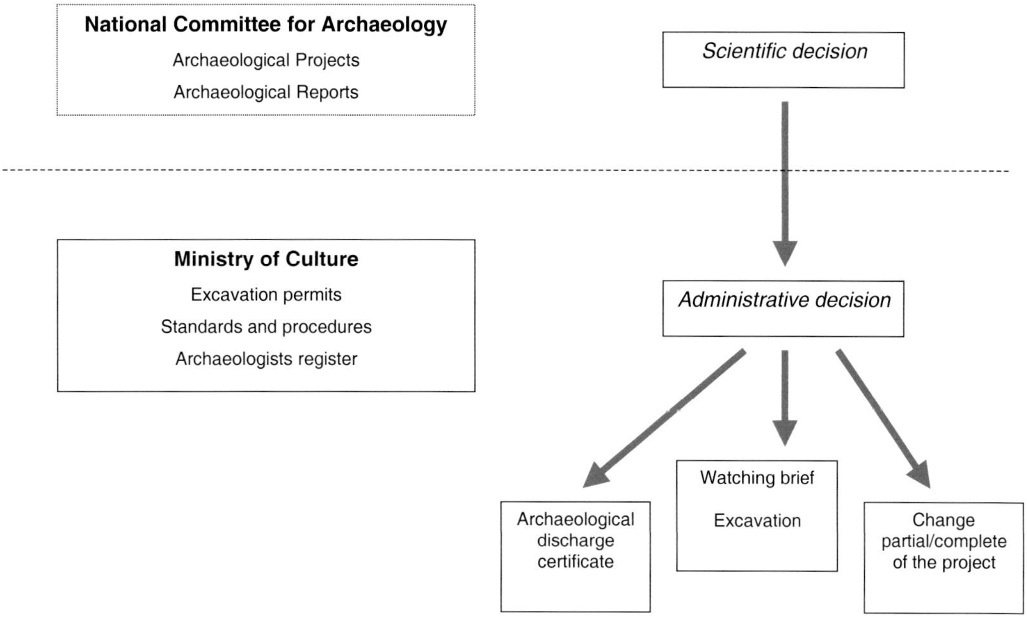

Figure 6.5 The division of tasks and responsibilities between the National Committee for Archaeology and the Ministry of Culture.

through the process of the research project in all stages and down to the final publication.

CONCLUSIONS

The reality of Romanian archaeology today imposes the need to apply a quality management system – the only way to obtain a uniform and coherent archaeological 'language'. The legal obligation to justify the way in which public money is spent, also implies a coherent system of reporting, even if many of the university based archaeologists have yet some difficulties in understanding this.

On the other hand this quality management system has been designed to offer an objective set of evaluation tools that allow for the quantification of the scientific efforts of the archaeologists by consistently using the same 'measurement units'.

Another important point that should be considered is, of course, compliance with the archaeological standards and procedures that may offer solutions (but not guarantees) for the cases when the archaeologist's work and its results is subject of action in the court of law.

One of the main results of the existence of standards is that this has allowed the creation of a national program for the inventory of archaeological sites, historical monuments and cultural landscape features (eGISpat, see Mihai 2005). Based on GIS technology, the results of this program will allow a better legal protection of the sites and a powerful tool for the management of the immovable archaeological heritage.

Of course, it must be stressed that compliance with this set of rules is intended to contribute to a growing public awareness – especially by instituting the obligation for archaeological reports to be communicated to the general public. Public access to excavations, creating special exhibitions, and various different methods for 'marketing' archaeology, all have their place in this system. Each community, no matter how big or small, assuming responsibility for an archaeological site on its territory is thereby assuming responsibility for its own past and that is to be considered as the main source for support that is to be granted to archaeology. The time of academic research that is done only for the specialist is gone. Starting with archaeological reports all work must be distributed as widely as possible and this is the only way that will convince the public of the social importance of our profession. From this point of view, the quality management system of Romanian archaeology can also be seen as a first step toward the opening to the public.

All these three management 'tools' will be maintained. Of course, when necessary they will be adapted to the ever changing circumstances of Romanian archaeology or when new methods and techniques will be developed. Whenever the profession will impose it, they will be customised and improved – hopefully – by the contribution of all archaeologists.

The recently introduced procedures of the Environmental Impact Assessment and the Strategic Impact Assessment, with the aim to identify and assess the direct and indirect effects of a development project on the soil, water, air, climate and the landscape, as well as on the material assets and the cultural heritage, will help to increase the scale of the way we are looking at the archaeological heritage. We are obliged to take into account the interaction between the factors mentioned above. Establishing standards, partnerships, strategies and policies for an integrated management and protection system, together with the governmental agencies involved in these processes, is a new challenge for Romanian archaeology of the coming years.

References

Angelescu, M. (2005) *Archaeological Standards and Procedures.* Bucharest.

Council of Europe (1985) *Convention for the Protection of the Architectural Heritage of Europe.* (European Treaty Series 121). Strasbourg.

Council of Europe (1992) *European Convention on the Protection of the Archaeological Heritage (revised).* (European Treaty Series 143). Strasbourg.

Council of Europe (2000) *European Landscape Convention.* (European Treaty Series 176). Strasbourg.

Council of Europe (2005) *Framework Convention on the Value of Cultural Heritage for Society.* (European Treaty Series 199). Strasbourg.

Mihai, D. (2005) The inventory of the Historic Monuments – Bilant i perspective, *Buletinul Monumentelor Istorice, an XII–XVI,* 1, 269–273.

World Intellectual Property Organization (1886) *Berne Convention for the Protection of Literary and Artistic Works.* Bern.

CHAPTER 7

Always fluid: government policy making and standards of practice in Ontario archaeological resource management

Neal Ferris

INTRODUCTION

It is little more than cliché now to point out that the rise and dominance of that particular form of archaeology known as archaeological resource management, (ARM), commercial or consulting archaeology has changed the face and fabric of the practice (*e.g.* Ferris 1998, 2002; Fowler 1995; Green and Doershuk 1998; Smith 2004). Certainly this *is* the archaeology the vast majority of professionals, students and the public experience day to day, and increasingly is the supply of data from which graduate students and established scholars rely on for in-depth research.

In Canada, the legislative authority for archaeology is delegated to the jurisdiction of the 10 provinces and 3 territories (Burley 1994; Turnbull 1977). In Ontario, this responsibility emerges from the Ontario Heritage Act (OHA), which requires all archaeological fieldwork to be done by individuals holding archaeological licenses issued by the Minister, who serves as the political head of the ministry responsible for the Act, most currently known as the Ministry of Culture. The OHA was enacted in 1975. In addition to licensing requirements, the Act also requires licensees to report on their field activities, adhere to the terms and conditions of their licenses, and care, in perpetuity, archaeological collections (artefacts and records) generated under those licenses (Ferris 1998). Until recently, the OHA remained largely unaltered from its original 1975 iteration. In other words, the regulatory regime for archaeology in Ontario was defined in the decade *before* the emergence of commercial ARM activities, and largely was conceived from within the needs and priorities of mid 1970s academic and avocational archaeological interests of the day (Noble 1982).

The province of Ontario is a very large land mass that has been characterised recently by a sustained, post World War II-period of intensive population growth and infrastructure development around intensively farmed rural areas – but mostly restricted to a 50–100 km wide swath east and north of the Great Lakes and St. Lawrence River along the Canadian-American border (figure 7.1). Beyond that zone the province is characterised by an extensive forestry industry, some mining and tourism development, and much smaller population centres.

The archaeological record in Ontario extends some 13,000 years or so, with humans living here for as long as humans could, beginning immediately following the retreat of glacial ice sheets, which happened first in the lower Great Lakes region (*e.g.* Ellis and Ferris 1990). The record is extremely rich and includes several

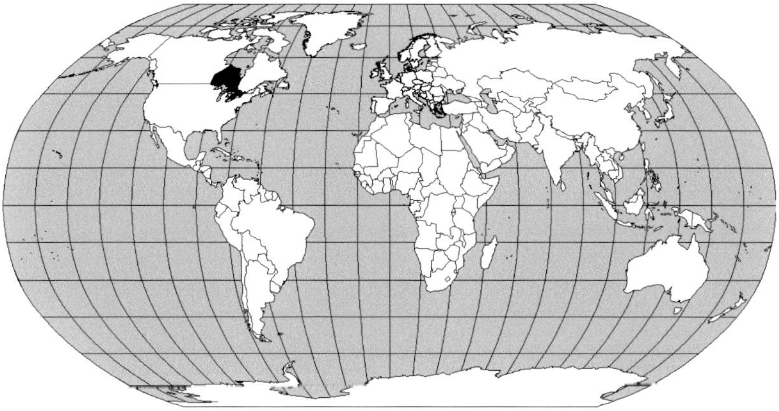

Figure 7.1 Where in the world is Ontario, Canada?

thousand years of seasonally mobile hunter and forager communities, followed by the rise of larger community aggregates and the emergence of Neolithic-like agricultural village and outlier settlement, Aboriginal sacred sites, as well as the Aboriginal and non-Aboriginal archaeology of the last half millennium representing frontier, pioneer, colonial and urban settlement occupations of the region (figure 7.2). The history of the archaeological pursuit of this record in Ontario over the last forty years in particular has been about our collective efforts and failures to identify, document and excavate these archaeological sites that otherwise would be destroyed and lost by the massive and large-scale growth and development that has occurred and continues to occur in the region.

LEGISLATING ARCHAEOLOGICAL CONSERVATION

Ontario archaeologists have been very successful in the single-minded pursuit of ensuring the protection or conservation of archaeological sites and resources. At first this took the form of an archaeological 'bureaucracy' (Noble 1982): archaeologists employed mostly by the Ministry of Culture (in whatever earlier iteration) who promoted archaeological awareness and conservation and advanced the aims of archaeology to policy and lawmakers inside the provincial government, municipalities and with the private sector development community (MacLeod 1977). As well, through the late 1970s and early 1980s government archaeologists also ended up acting as a kind of archaeological salvage/rescue force, responding to reports of sites under threat from bulldozers and development. Relying too much on volunteers, these efforts led to either massive successes, recovering ancient native

Figure 7.2 The archaeology of Ontario is dominated by the history and material of indigenous peoples who developed traditions and ways of life over the millennia (Photo Karen Matilla, Longwoods Road Conservation Area).

village sites and contributing to the advancement of academic knowledge (*e.g.* Fox 1980; Timmins 1997), or humiliating failures, as reflected in headlines such as "Bulldozers put end to Huron village dig" (Globe and Mail, September 10th 1984). In effect, what that period taught government archaeologists and policy makers alike was that there would always be more sites threatened by impact than government staff to salvage them (Ferris 1998; see also Fox 1990; Ogilvie 1990).

And the unprecedented scale of development was certainly swallowing up a significant portion of the archaeological record in Ontario (*e.g.* Coleman and Williamson 1994). So between 1975 and 1985, a number of provincial land use and development statutes were revised to, among other things, capture the need to conserve archaeological resources as part of their development approval processes. The Environmental Assessment Act first articulated a requirement to conserve archaeological sites in the late 1970s, while in the early 1980s the Planning Act also identified archaeology as a provincial interest that had to be accounted for in development decisions (Ferris 1998). By the late 1990s these requirements had expanded to other legislation, and received broader application within the environmental assessment and planning processes (Ferris 2002). As a result, strong requirements for archaeological conservation are now achieved in a multitude of land use statutes, ranging from major and minor public infrastructure undertakings such as highways, power transmission corridors and energy pipelines, landfills, municipal roads and water/wastewater projects, to private land development of residential housing, commercial, industrial or recreational facilities, to resource extraction for quarries and forestry. This legislative regime can even identify and trigger conservation requirements for small-scale undertakings, such as a single residential lot development or municipal park landscaping (Ontario Ministry of Culture 1997).

The general process for achieving conservation within these various legislated land use processes requires that land proposed for development be evaluated for a host of historic and physical features that collectively will suggest if the land in question has the 'potential' for containing any of the range of archaeological sites present in Ontario. These features, or 'screening criteria', rely heavily on landscape features such as the location and proximity to present and ancient watercourses and topography, as well as known site locations and non-Aboriginal settlement patterns, to determine potential (see OMC 1997). These criteria are either 'specialised' – informed by a modelling exercise undertaken by an archaeologist – or 'generalised' – developed by the Ministry of Culture for use by non-specialists (*e.g.* municipal planners), and thus operating at more of a simple yes-no light switch to determine whether or not the land need be assessed by a qualified archaeologist.

When reviewing a specific parcel of land, if features of potential indicate that archaeological sites may be present, the development proponent is required to have the subject property archaeologically surveyed and assessed. This consists of a documentary pre-survey check of information about the property (stage 1) so as to inform survey methodologies and coverage, a systematic field survey being conducted across the entire property (stage 2), and a site-specific assessment (surface and below surface test excavation and mapping) of the cultural heritage value for all sites found (stage 3). The Ministry of Culture reviews the findings of this work, along with any recommendations (stage 4) for significant sites to be either preserved *in situ*, or excavated in advance of development (figure 7.3, figure 7.4). Once all relevant stages have been completed, the ministry will sign off on the archaeology, waiving protection provisions for site locales fully excavated or deemed at that point to have been adequately documented, and so allowing the approval authority to clear the archaeological requirement tied to the development to enable construction or extraction.

Critically, the twin implications underlining this process, that not all development properties will have archaeological potential (though typically 60–80% do), and that sites found can be excavated by an archaeologist and so be physically removed in order to allow development to proceed, proved to be key principles that were crucial during the 1980s and 1990s in 'selling' the idea that archaeological conservation could work within development approval processes. In other words, archaeology

Figure 7.3 Excavations of Late Woodland, Neolithic-like settlements, revealed features like the outline of structures such as an Iroquoian longhouse (Photo Ontario Ministry of Culture).

was not a constraint to development, but was something to be addressed in the process of completing development (Ferris 2000, 2004).

THE EMERGENCE OF A 'NEW' ARCHAEOLOGICAL PROFESSION

The imposition of these archaeological conservation requirements, and the Ontario Heritage Act requirement for all archaeological fieldwork to be conducted by someone holding an archaeological license, means that the developer requires the services of a specialist contracted to undertake the work. And as government archaeologists in Ontario moved back from directly undertaking these studies, a new form of archaeologist – the private sector commercial or consultant archaeologist – emerged in Ontario in the 1980s (Ferris 1998; Tyyska 1986). Over time, this industry, or business, or part of the archaeological discipline (differing opinions have decidedly different considerations for what it means to be a consultant archaeologist), has become a viable and permanent livelihood for many, although there is significant disparity in salary, security and benefits depending on the particular firm someone happens to be employed by.

These days, between 150 and 200 individuals are mostly employed over the course of the year in consulting archaeology in Ontario, and seasonally another 200

Figure 7.4 Iroquoian longhouse (Photo Ontario Ministry of Culture).

to 300 people are employed over the field season, which runs from late February to December in the south-western part of the province. The consulting industry generates, at best guess, somewhere in the neighbourhood of $15–20 million Canadian dollars annually in revenues. At present, just under 60 archaeological consulting firms compete for this business, and range from storefront operations employing over 50 individuals undertaking two to three hundred projects a year, to one person-spare bedroom operations doing less than half a dozen projects a year.

The integration of this conservation strategy into land use development activities meant that when the sustained economic development in this region of the world began in the mid-1990s, the standardised requirement for archaeology tied to these activities led to an explosion of archaeological consulting activity, which continues unabated. And this explosion of work over the last decade has all been uniformly serviced by this new breed of private sector archaeologist-for-hire. Figure 7.5, for example, illustrates that in each of the last 10 years the number of individual projects consultants have undertaken in Ontario has increased every year, and has quadrupled between 1966 (364 projects) and 2005 (1499 projects). Indeed, in 2005, 341 site-specific excavations were undertaken by consultant archaeologists, almost equalling the entire PIF output from 1996. Typically each year about 80% of these

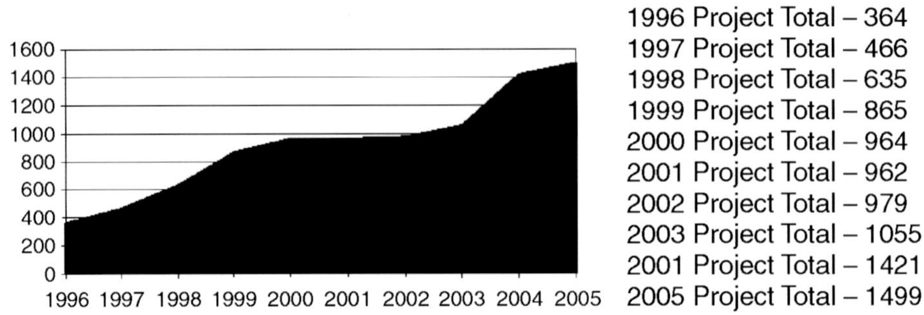

Figure 7.5 Total of individual projects (confirmed through submission of project information forms) undertaken by all Ontario consultant archaeologists, 1996–2005.

projects occur in less than a fourth of the province's landmass, within that region of Ontario referred to as south-central and south-western Ontario, extending from the broad Toronto region along western Lake Ontario, to Windsor at the west end of Lake Erie.

The scale of what is happening in Ontario is also reflected in the annual numbers of archaeological sites documented. Over 9500 sites have been registered over the last 16 years, or just under 600 sites a year. About 85% of all these sites are directly the result of ARM activity (figure 7.6). Given that the sites found by ARM contexts are on lands that will be completely altered by construction activities, this percentage represents that part of the archaeological record that would have been lost had archaeological conservation requirements not existed. Moreover, this work has qualitatively changed the substance and breadth of Ontario's archaeological record, because development review means full land coverage. As a result, ARM archaeology documents the whole cultural-temporal range of the record present in Ontario, including site types previously little investigated, documented or understood by the research community.

FROM CATCH-AS-CATCH-CAN EXPEDIENCIES TO TECHNICAL GUIDELINES

While the growth of Ontario's archaeological consulting industry and the resulting scale of resource documentation have certainly been substantial, it has also been a mixed blessing. In particular since the archaeological community (inside or outside government) never really anticipated what the changes would be once they convinced lawmakers to recognise the importance of archaeological conservation, they generally haven't been prepared to deal with the problems associated with

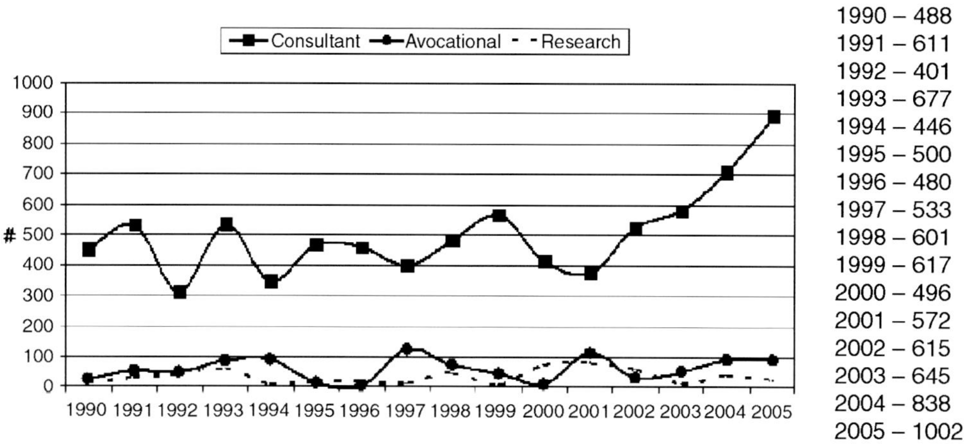

Figure 7.6 Total number of new sites by year, registered by archaeologists in the province of Ontario 1990–2005.

these changes. As well, consultant archaeologists (and perhaps the government archaeologists that work with them) have emerged as a unique type of archaeologist, working in a largely uncharted dimension of the practice, negotiating a set of demands and expectations of professional practice not faced by any other breed of archaeologist, and which arise from having to interpret and meet legislated standards of archaeological practice and land use development, expectations of their profession, regulators and development clients, and their own desire to 'do good' archaeology while also obtaining job satisfaction, professional affirmation, and meaningful livelihood. All of these tensions are manifest in almost every decision these practitioners make each day, which has made it hard over the last couple of decades to focus on broader issues, or solutions that advance the practice, rather than serve transitory self-interests.

Without a map or rulebook to negotiate this uncharted dimension of the practice, consultant archaeologists initially felt their way through, relying on intuition, expediency, and ministry support and informal friendships to determine judgements, methodologies and practices (Tyyska 1986). While this generally worked effectively for the first wave of consultant archaeologists in the practice, it also generated a highly variable set of practices and philosophies that operated purely subjectively, substantiated only by assertions of personal opinion and limited experience. These sets of practices were also largely unspoken and informal agreements between a handful of consultants and government reviewers – dispositions that 'made sense' only as long as those personalities were solely the ones involved in the decision-making.

As early as the late 1980s the ARM community (private sector and government) had collectively compiled a host of experiences that severely questioned the appropriateness of individual strategies and methodologies, and the 'fairness' of agreements made at the individual consultant to individual government archaeologist level (*e.g.* Adams 1986; Stewart 1986). What emerged at the time was a growing recognition that these informal, subjective catch as catch can strategies needed some 'corralling' into clearer standards, practices and expectations. Moreover it was clear that this really had to emerge from the archaeological community itself (*i.e.* as codes of practice and requirements tied to archaeological licenses), and not from within the development processes archaeology had been woven into. The distinction was critical because while regulated land use activities in Ontario required archaeology to be addressed as part of development undertakings, none of these statutes said anything about the *quality* of the archaeology to be done, just that it had to be done (Ferris 1998).

So, as the ARM industry first began to grow and impact on a wider part of the province's development sector, the lack of clear, arbitrary standards, articulated expectations of practice, and codified definitions of professionalism all created a massive void between 'doing archaeology' and 'doing archaeology right'. That archaeologists were filling the void with a decade of idiosyncratic, reactive solutions to particular contingencies in many ways left the public required to pay for archaeological conservation wondering if the whole practice wasn't just made up (Ferris 1999, 2004). And variable practices also began to undermine the faith of archaeologists earnestly working towards the conservation of the resource, leading them to question why they should try and do a 'good' job, when there were so many instances of perceived or real unprofessional behaviour on the part of some of their colleagues, including underbidding and use of sub-standard practices that government reviewers were then cajoled into accepting (*e.g.* Adams 1994; Ferris 2000; Parker 1996; Williamson 2000).

Recognition of the need to fill the void, in the minds of many archaeologists, clearly had to arise from the articulation of standards of practice – the quality assurances that prevent idiosyncratic practices and avoids rewarding underbidding achieved through sub-standard methodologies. Efforts by the archaeological community began to take form by the late 1980s. In 1987 archaeologists met at a government sponsored workshop to review the need for technical standards of practice. Subsequent detailed questionnaires on a host of technical details filled out by consultants were then compiled and presented back to the community at a workshop held a year later (Ferris 1988). During that meeting a series of consensus statements emerged and were formally voted on. These then formed the basis of articulated stage 1–3 assessment standards, and the reporting of that activity. In other words, formalised standards of practice emerged internally from commonly understood, in-the-field methodologies articulated and agreed to by the community of the day actively engaged in undertaking that work. Archaeologists who favoured either more or less than the consensus were effectively marginalised from these benchmarks. While bureaucratic will and complaints meant the standards remained draft for several years afterwards, they were formally implemented in 1993 (Ontario Ministry of Culture 1993). Stage 4 guidelines were not developed at the time for fear that they were too complex and would delay implementation of the other standards.

When these standards were adopted, all licensed archaeologists doing commercial archaeology were required to adhere to them. This was imposed by making adherence a condition on all licenses to allowed fieldwork for the purposes of commercial conservation activities. The guide itself is 12 pages long, and provides a limited number of explicit statements wrapped in a language of broad guidance for professional consultants to understand the 'typical' expectations of practice, along with more detailed technical standards. Typical statements reflecting the range of directive include:

- 'Assessments shall not be conducted under weather conditions which can inhibit the identification of sites and/or will result in the loss of data or damage to cultural material. For example, no surface surveys shall be conducted on lands covered by snow and no test pit surveys shall be conducted on ground frozen 3 cm or more below surface.' (Ontario Ministry of Culture 1993, 4)
- 'Sites found during test pitting will require excavating an intensified test pit grid around the artefact yielding pit (2.5 m interval or less). All fill will be screened, and test pits within the intensified grid mapped (both artefact yielding and negative), and tied into a permanent datum.' (Ontario Ministry of Culture 1993, 6)
- 'All artefact recoveries shall be bagged in the conventional manner and documented according to provenience (*e.g.* surface locality, or transect line and test pit number). In the lab artefacts should be processed in accordance with standard procedures for cleaning and cataloguing. Minimally, all artefacts or batches of artefacts must be clearly labelled with the Borden Number assigned to the site.' (Ontario Ministry of Culture 1993, 7)

In effect what this document captured was the ARM community's understanding of how archaeology should be done in these commercial conservation contexts to recover all 'important' dimensions of the archaeological record present within development properties, based on their experiences over the proceeding decade in the 1980s. The guidelines also provided a level of clarity these *existing* practitioners felt was necessary to ensure they all were doing, broadly, the same thing in order to achieve the same outcome, *i.e.* discovery and conservation of Ontario's archaeological heritage as known and considered important at that point in the history of the discipline. Through the 1990s it became clear that these standards did advance practices and regularise expectations for basic survey and site evaluation, so that certainly the more egregious of past idiosyncratic practices (*e.g.* surveying snow covered fields or use of irregular test pit survey intervals) disappeared.

But it was also the case that through the 1990s, especially in the face of dramatic increases in the range, type and setting of ARM projects being done across the entirety of the province, that continued contingencies and consultants pushing the envelope of expectations generated a sister, 'ghost' set of standards, which by common memory and experience bred a series of 'what ifs' and 'yes, buts' and 'in situation x method y is an ok alternative'. Implicit was that none of these ghost standards were formally articulated, just informally negotiated on a case by case basis between individual private sector archaeologists and their ministry counterparts. And as the industry grew and bureaucratic archaeologists changed, these less than rules became the dispositions to a sort of archaeological *habitus* known only by a select few, while the mysterious, unknown and unfair justifications for turning back reports or losing bids for other, more novice consultants.

So the inevitable happened over the 1990s. Despite a set of 'standards', highly variable practices emerged among consultant and government archaeologists. And by the late 1990s the scale of consulting and its fiscal and scheduling impact on development was proving much more significant than a decade earlier. So as a consequence, when the fallout of these variable practices began to be felt in the form of complaints and threats of legal action, the ARM community generally, and Ministry of Culture specifically, found itself defending this encyclopaedic range of informal variations to practice, inconsistent precedents, and widely divergent understandings of standards and process requirements among individual consultants.

More critically, given the wider and more substantial extent of archaeological conservation regimes within legislated land use processes by this time, ARM activities began to rise 'above the radar' of policy and political staff, typically as a result of complaints about the burden this conservation impulse placed on proponents who had to pay for this activity, made by influential members of the provincial development sector or from politicians sympathetic to the complaint (Ferris 2004). And when these complaints went beyond blatant self interest to point to variable costs attributed to variable practices carried out by different consultants or enforced by different bureaucratic archaeologists, the complaints resonated with senior management. Consequently, inside government bureaucratic archaeologists were increasingly required to justify what appeared to be manufactured standards and associated costs for either specific elements of conservation processes, or for the entire program itself, to political advocates of the development sector, senior management, and political staff of the governing cabinet. This, combined with the lack of stage 4 guidelines contributing to radically differing excavation strategies and costs for the same kind of site, sometimes paid for by the same proponent, led to the whole conservation regime to be criticised as either a bureaucratic fiefdom or select consultant playground to exploit development monies. Status quo was clearly challenged when people like the Minister of Culture's own Executive Assistant called archaeological program and management staff up to his office and suggested to that staff that consulting archaeology was nothing more than a boondoggle for their buddies in the private sector.

At about the same time government archaeologists found themselves increasingly in dispute with particular consultant archaeologists over differences in the quality of work done, value of sites to be conserved, and more generally over the 'right' of government archaeologists to second guess the 'professional' judgement and competitive business practices of these private sector archaeologists. In some cases more novice consultants who were not part of the past unspoken understanding of the way things worked, increasingly framed their objections to the managers and politicians in the Ministry of Culture as one of persecution: ministry archaeological staff were rejecting their work because of personal favouritism or because they chose to put their clients' needs ahead of the personal or selfish 'archaeological research' interests of competitors who were friends to those bureaucrat archaeologists.

Ultimately, in 1998 these consultants and their development clients took their complaints – both self-serving and philosophical – to the provincial Red Tape Commission, a committee of backbench politicians from the ruling, conservative-oriented provincial government of the day created specifically to hear business-sector complaints of government bureaucracy that was felt to impede the pursuit of free enterprise. As a result, the entire ARM program that had emerged over the preceding two decades was being second-guessed, and management in the ministry felt exposed to the criticism, unable to defend such an informal, undefined structure operating far beyond any policy direction.

To deflect these criticisms and to assuage the Red Tape Commission, ministry management agreed to undertake a comprehensive review of provincial archaeology programs. In addition, management began to increasingly curtail the role ministry archaeological staff could play in either the program review or in continued independent decision-making when it came to archaeological program direction. This was less an overt decision and more a general shift in the culture of the ministry, and did not preclude generalist policy staff from working with program staff. However, there was a general sense that the ministry's problems with the Red Tape Commission, and the complaints from a handful of consultants levelled against individual staff, were somehow all the 'fault' of archaeological staff. While there is no doubt that staff contributed to some of the tensions occurring in the late 1990s by critically reviewing consultant work and holding them to largely unarticulated standards and process expectations, it is also true that the disputes with the consultants in question were over practices that were also clearly at variance with the practices of the broader community. The inability of staff to otherwise address these concerns effectively arose more from systemic deficiencies in the ministry-led process, than from the individual personalities involved. While this is largely recognised as being the case today, once that culture of blame took hold inside management in the ministry, archaeological program staff have continued to remain isolated from most corporate decision-making, and even deliberations, about the direction archaeological programs should follow.

THE ARCHAEOLOGICAL CUSTOMER SERVICE PROJECT

The program review that management had committed to undertake, began in 2000 and was termed the Ministry of Culture's Archaeological Customer Service Project. The stated objectives of this overhaul to archaeological programs in Ontario have been:

1. to recognize provincial responsibility for protection and preservation of Ontario's heritage;
2. to ensure transparent and fair business practices and high customer service standards;
3. to encourage conditions for the consultant archaeologist and development industries to prosper by removing unnecessary regulatory barriers;
4. to recognize that consultant archaeology is carried out by trained professionals capable of operating with an appropriate degree of autonomy.

The clear emphasis in this review has been on archaeology as a commercial enterprise, and seeking to revise consultant industry practices and the ministry's role in affecting consultants and their development proponents. Indeed, it is fair to say that the motivations of development sector complainants to the Red Tape Commission clearly included seeing a reduction in the burden of archaeological conservation costs to that sector, while the consultant archaeologist complainants were clearly seeking to reduce or eliminate the ministry's role in regulating the practice, through the delegation of all responsibilities for archaeology onto individual consultants.

While the formal language of the Red Tape Commission to the ministry never pushed these agendas outright, they clearly were sympathetic to programs shifting in those directions, and early discussions between the ministry and the Commission included repeated debates as to why archaeological conservation was even necessary and why proponents needed to pay for such things as the recovery of "road gravel" (*i.e.* lithic scatters). However, while eliminating the requirement or radically reducing the compliance dimension of archaeological conservation may have been toyed with by senior levels of management in the ministry, once policy staff began investigating the basis, range and scope of the statutory requirements and the implications this archaeological heritage conservation regime had to the province, and began speaking to people beyond staff and consultant complainants, they realised three critical points that quickly revised any agenda towards the reduction of elimination of the conservation regime or the ministry's role in the regime:

- First, it was immediately obvious that archaeological consultants did not enjoy a critical mass or financial capacity to self regulate;
- Second, as soon as policy advisors began exploring the program in detail, they discovered that the basic elements of the conservation process were effective, avoided costs associated with confrontation, and were supported broadly by archaeologists and even many in the development sector, and only really was undermined by complex issues and individual misunderstandings arising from unarticulated expectations;

Figure 7.7 In the mid 1980s Ontario Ministry of Culture staff investigated the looting of a 17th century Iroquoian cemetery. The results of this investigation led to the first successful prosecution under the Ontario Heritage Act of the individuals who looted this burial ground (Photo Ontario Ministry of Culture).

- Third, by the late 1990s Ontario's diverse Aboriginal communities had begun to voice strong concerns for the management of their archaeological heritage. While focussed mostly on burial issues (figure 7.7), increasingly these groups objected to developments if they felt archaeology had not been accounted for or if the commercial archaeology work done was felt to be sub-standard (Ferris 2003).

Since ARM programs and processes could not be eliminated or delegated out of the ministry, then the direction of the ACSP increasingly shifted towards addressing systemic deficiencies of past practices by formally articulating standards, best practices, and laying out expectations for all those involved. These efforts have centred on two dimensions of archaeological programs – the licensing of archaeologists (*i.e.* defining professionalism), and revising the existing technical guidelines for consultants into a more comprehensive set of standards and guidelines.

'PROFESSIONALISM' DEFINED

Licensing was an obvious area that needed to be overhauled, since this was the basis by which archaeologists could assert their professional credentials to do commercial archaeology. However, the basis for obtaining a license had never been defined and very idiosyncratic practices in the Ministry in accommodating individual variation over the previous 25 years had created a multitude of pseudo-categories of license (consultant, consultant stage 2 or 3 only, consultant stage 2 and 3 full, stage 4 historic only, consultant industrial archaeology only, etc.). So a critical first task was to differentiate categories of competency and activity that would accommodate differences between consultant and avocational archaeologists, or project and field directors working on commercial projects. While the discussion and debate over licensing dominated ACSP efforts in the early years, and the formal regulation enacting the new license categories was only adopted in 2006, in the end the ministry adopted a distinction in category and eligibility consistent with other jurisdictions: a Professional category license eligibility included quantitative and qualitative criteria of past experience and education (*e.g.* thesis MA and 52 weeks past field experience), an Applied Researcher category for field directors, graduate students and senior avocationals had a reduced set of eligibility criteria (BA and 30 weeks experience, or 5 years experience for senior avocationals), and a general Avocational category requiring minimal qualifications.

Critically, the Professional License category of license defined, for the first time, how an individual could substantiate their claim to being a professional archaeologist. And, in the logic of the ACSP, Professional Licensees, because of meeting a higher qualification benchmark, could also be given greater latitude from ministry scrutiny, under the assumption that the ministry no longer would need to impose the personal opinion of technical staff onto the professional opinion of a qualified consultant archaeologist. In short, while the ACSP recognised that self-regulation of the private sector archaeological community was not viable, this was so in part because professional qualifications had never been stipulated.

That benchmark has now been established. However, the fact that all individuals holding comparable licenses under the old regime in the years 2000 and 2001 were grandparented into the professional category (regardless of their educational or field experience background), while serving a political expediency, has also meant that any supposed 'raising of the bar' of professionalism will be a long transition and motivated by the individual professional impulses of these grandparented licensees, rather than because of re-training or a weeding out of under-qualified practitioners.

FROM TECHNICAL GUIDELINES TO PROFESSIONAL STANDARDS OF PRACTICE

The second major undertaking of the ACSP, and one that continues to the present, arose form the recognition that articulated standards of practice, creating clear and specific expectations on the part of all directly and indirectly affected by ARM activities, had to be generated through the thorough revision and expansion of the existing technical guidelines.

While the need for expanded technical standards had been seen as an essential next step in moving towards a maturing of the profession long before the inception of the ACSP, developing them has proven to be a monumental task of rediscovering the obvious. In fact the adoption of the earlier technical guidelines in 1993 specifically recognised that a more comprehensive set of technical guidelines for stage 4 mitigation still had to be developed. And towards that end, in the mid 1990s the archaeological programs portion of the ministry had hosted a workshop on the technical guidelines and determined a broad number of themes that still had to be developed to define and articulate a comprehensive set of standards of practice. The archaeology program developed a detailed questionnaire covering everything from investigating find spots during stage 2 work, to stage 4 excavation and protection standards, to artefact care and documentation, to participation of descendant populations in ARM activities. This was sent out in 1996 to 110 ARM archaeologists, academics and avocationals, and the ministry received back 54 responses. These had been compiled and the results were being reported back to the archaeological community in 1998 in advance of developing a draft set of standards for consultation, when the events that birthed the ACSP supplanted that initiative.

Under the aegis of the ACSP, the ministry itself at first had difficulty deciding which way to proceed. As this program review was being led almost exclusively by ministry policy staff who wanted to rely heavily on the notion that professional archaeologists did not need the ministry telling them what to do, the impulse of policy staff initially was to develop a very short, 2 to 5 page document that would articulate broad statements defining what 'good' archaeology should entail. Ministry archaeological staff objected that such a strategy would not clarify expectations and lead to even greater variable practices and disagreements between ministry staff and private sector consultants. But as program staff was considered the problem that necessitated the ACSP, their concerns were not given much credence.

However, over the first two years of the ACSP policy staff undertook several external program reviews, and all those studies came back suggesting that the issues were much more complex than the motherhood statements policy staff had hoped to adopt could allow for. Moreover, initial policy staff meetings with the 'customers', *i.e.* consultant archaeologists, were disastrous in that the technical details which seemed so trivial to policy staff became the focus of heated debates during the consultations. Eventually, it was recognised that some limited in-house staff archaeological expertise was needed to both inform policy, and 'morally legitimise' the program review to private-sector archaeologists.

At about the same time, another external study done for the project on the nature of standards and guidelines was completed and significantly changed the internal thinking on what the function and aim of standards and guidelines should be. The study pointed out that the 1993 standards proved most effective in establishing clear and standardised expectations of practice when the document provided detailed qualitative technical statements. The document engendered variable and conflicting assumptions of practice, however, when only broad, general statements of intent were provided. Because of this the study recommended the new standards incorporate much more detailed qualitative statements to ensure comprehensive clarity around expectations and quality assurances. It also pointed out that having detailed standards would establish clear, easily demonstrated expectations of outcomes that would then significantly reduce the effort required of ministry staff to review resultant reports. In other words, reduce ministry workload and involvement to a focussed review and rubber stamping the results of clear expectations carried out by professional archaeologists operating from detailed standards of practice and articulated outcomes.

As such, over the last 4 years the ministry has developed a very detailed set of standards and guidelines covering the 'universe' of ARM practices, ranging from field activities to artefact analysis, care and reporting. It also has outlined the parameters and limits of the ministry review process that would occur under this new regime, to convey clear expectations for consultant and ministry staff, as well as developers and third party interests, of how the process would work. This undertaking followed the 1993 guideline process by defining standards initially from questionnaire feedback, in this case from the 1996 questionnaire. The drafting of the document consisted of a staff archaeologist generating raw text that was heavily revised by policy staff, and then reviewed by the entire archaeological unit. The resulting first draft was a blend of archaeological detail, policy constraint, and 'plain language' format that reflected a non-specialist's sensibilities.

This draft, once approved by management, was then 'tested' to a focus group of consultants and other archaeologists (a Technical Advisory Group, or TAG), who were asked to provide feedback and general comment to help revise and refine the document. While policy staff initially hoped the exercise would stick to general-level comments, and tried to shape the feedback from TAG members to conform to this expectation, the TAG archaeologists were much more interested in a line by line review and detailed discussion and debate over technical particulars. The meetings thus were long and involved, and proved much more enjoyable for the archaeologists than for policy staff, who lamented often at the slow pace of the review and the seemingly arcane, technical jargon that dominated discussion. TAG discussion also tended to shift particular standards back in the direction that ministry archaeological staff had originally favoured but had been overruled by policy preference. For example, based on questionnaire feedback, the initial, internal draft of the document indicated that test pits dug during survey had to be 30 cm in diameter and dug to subsoil. When policy staff read this statement they eliminated it, saying that it was far too detailed a direction and archaeologists would be insulted to be told how to dig a hole. Yet when this section of the document was reviewed by TAG they were unanimous that a statement of size and depth had to be included, to avoid the practice of 'divot pits' all claimed other archaeologists practiced.

Indeed, the TAG process managed to significantly 'ratchet' up many technical benchmarks, as group dynamics of the discussions often led to a consensus for whatever was perceived to be 'best' for the resource or 'raised the bar' for the practice. Cost implications were not considered a legitimate concern, though subsequent, wider consultation has led to some of these standards being toned down.

Over 2004 and 2005, as first the fieldwork and then reporting, artefact analysis and ministry review process sections of the document went through the TAG review, the ministry initiated a process of further consultation with the wider archaeological community on the TAG-approved draft. Feedback from this broader consultation has ranged from indifference ("I do that already") to outrage, and suspicion that the TAG group itself had been pursuing ulterior agendas. Indeed, the extraordinary length of time it has taken the ministry to undertake this task (given that it pre-dated the inception of the ACSP by five years), has bred a distrust about what the ministry's intentions have been, and has tended to mean that every ACSP announcement triggers a flurry of objections and letters that re-directs ministry staff efforts for a time.

In general, most archaeologists have welcomed the proposed, more constrained ministry review process proposed in the Standards and Guidelines, but generally can find one or several statements in the document constraining to *themselves*. A curious phenomenon is that most criticism has arisen over field survey methodologies, which really only reflect a continuation of the standards (and the methodological philosophy behind those standards) already articulated in the 1993 technical standards document. In fact, the criticisms appear to be a direct manifestation of the weaknesses that general, imprecise statements engender, since a careful examination of the criticism on these survey methodologies has revealed that a long standing practice from one part of the province administered by one ministry staff person was at odds with the original intent of the 1993 document. Specifically, an informal assumption grew up between that reviewer and the consultants who work in that area over the last decade that 'spot' survey was okay for areas the archaeologist intuitively *knew* a site would be. Systematic survey of all lands of potential, which is both the standard and the practice elsewhere in Ontario, was simply ignored in that region. So, in effect, a broad philosophical distinction emerged between the need to survey all lands that would be altered by development (what the 1993 document requires), and the assumption that an archaeologist did not have to survey lands they individually suspected would not contain sites (creating a much lower threshold for survey cost requirements). Thus the new Standards and Guidelines, though only affirming the 1993 intent of survey methodologies, was seen by practitioners in this one part of the province as an onerous, unwarranted constraint to their personal judgements, regardless of the fact that in practice their judgements, individually, varied significantly from each other.

This reaction reinforced the finding of the 2002 OMC internal study that the Standards and Guidelines, in order to operate beyond idiosyncratic variation, requires explicit expectations free from personal reinterpretation. It also suggests that any standards of practice adopted will require a continual review to ensure consistent delivery, or modification to reflect informed feedback from accumulated experiences.

But for some Ontario archaeologists the necessity for a comprehensive set of Standards and Guidelines to meet quality assurances remains anathema to the way they think archaeology works. For them, cookie-cutter practices cannot adequately capture the range of settings and resources archaeologists face on the landscape, and neuters professional, seasoned expertise and judgement. Ironically, in objecting to the nature or some of the details of the draft Standards and Guidelines, some archaeologists have tended to characterise the document as the *ministry's* standards and guidelines (*i.e.* foreign and imposed), despite the fact that the document, particularly at the level of technical detail, reflects the broad consensus of a practice the archaeological community articulated back to the ministry in various consultations and questionnaires. Indeed, in the wider consultation of the draft document, standards vilified by some archaeologists have been criticised as not stringent enough by other archaeologists. When this pointed out, objectors suggest those who say they are not dissatisfied with the standards are either not being truthful, or have ulterior motives (*i.e.* increasing fees to clients) to welcoming such onerous standards.

I would argue there is plenty of room in the proposed document for archaeologists to exercise judgement, and indeed the standards were specifically developed to be augmented by guidelines specifically to allow for more or less effort ('best practices') depending on that professional judgement. Nonetheless, there is no question that the imposition of the final version of the Standards and Guidelines in Ontario will significantly constrain past personal and informal preferences of practice.

CONCLUDING COMMENTS

Presently, the draft Standards and Guidelines have been significantly revised on the basis of the feedback received. They are currently being reviewed at a management level, and any further rounds of consultation, of a general or specific nature, is being contemplated. Most recently, First Nations and development sector interests have expressed a desire to have a hand in shaping the standards. How those sectors will be accommodated within the development of technical standards of practice for professional archaeologists is still not resolved. While any number of political realities or issues may detour both timing and content, the plan at present is to see the final version of the Standards and Guidelines released in 2006, to be operationalised by the start of the 2007 field season. Further critique and criticism is anticipated from those who want more and from those who want less and from those who do not want to be constrained at all. It is anticipated that the Standards and Guidelines will need to be revisited shortly after being operationalised (*i.e.* within one or two field seasons), to determine their impact and whether or not they are in fact achieving a consistent set of practices in Ontario.

In the end I anticipate that the arguments about the constraint to personal judgement these standards of practice will cause will ultimately proven to be moot. The issue is not what is or isn't the appropriate way to survey woodland or describe findings. Rather, the dramatic increase in commercial archaeology demands a rigour and quality assurance that rises above personal opinion, be it professional or inexperienced. It simply is no longer legitimate for a consultant to say they think a property should not be surveyed or site should not be excavated because they personally don't feel there are any archaeological concerns to worry about. Neither should ministry staff be able to demand much more excavation for a site type they personally find significant, even though most other archaeologists would not be willing to excavate. Simply put, ARM activities affects, and is on the radar of, too many interests and sectors in society today to expect the practices and requirements to arise internally and intangibly from the say so of practitioners, no matter how noble, or self serving, those sentiments may be.

Articulated and detailed standards deliver a degree of quality assurance that non-archaeologists – developer or descendant community – can see as the formal expectation when documenting the past. Any dispute or challenge is then about those standards, not about the opinion of an individual archaeologist. Indeed, it is not too much of a stretch to see these standardised expectations (and associated costs) as being where the sometimes conflicting interests of economic development and First Nations rights, at least with respect to the Aboriginal heritage in Ontario, will be mediated (Ferris 2003, 2004).

To most archaeologists in Ontario, either directly or indirectly, there is a growing recognition that what formal standards and quality assurance are about is actually the maturing of the discipline, and accountability *beyond* the discipline. And with the establishment of these standards, it could also be argued that the ministry, in many ways, will have reached the limits of its ability to effectively and competently manage or police archaeological practice. This is because, with fully articulated standards of practice and definitions of professional capacity, the ministry's role in the conservation process will increasingly be only to parrot those standards back to a professional archaeological community mostly adhering to them. At that point, archaeologists likely will be better placed to address further issues facing practitioners. So, in the end, these foundational steps of defining professionalism and quality assurance may well serve to advance the original ACSP sympathies of a reduced ministry role in the practice and the emergence of formal self-regulation. It is at this point that archaeologists will then be able to be truly accountable to both themselves and the rest of society being impacted by the imposition of conservation requirements, and most effectively demonstrate the value of archaeology as something beneficial beyond the archaeologist's own personal interest and employment.

ACKNOWLEDGEMENTS

I would like to thank my colleagues in the Ministry of Culture who work so tirelessly to continually seek to further enhance the appreciation and conservation of Ontario's archaeological heritage. I would also like to thank my archaeological brethren in Ontario beyond the ministry, who also work so passionately for their discipline, the resource, and for all those who care, or should care, about Ontario's archaeological heritage. While many would refuse to accept it, it is simple fact that almost all the people in these two halves strive for many of the same goals and concerns – intent just gets lost in translation too often. Despite, or because of this, I stress that the opinions and observations offered here are entirely my own personal take on matters, and in no way begins to reflect the views, positions or policies of my employer, management, colleagues or fellow archaeologists.

References

Adams, N. (1986) Block "D": Assessment by Legislation. In W. Fox (ed.) *Archaeological Consulting in Ontario: Papers of the London Conference 1985*, 3–8. (Occasional Publications of the London Chapter, Ontario. Archaeological Society, Number 2, 69–72). London/Ontario.

Adams, N. (1994) Gnawing Gently on the Metacarpals. *Arch Notes* 94 (1), 9–15.

Burley, D. (1994) A Never Ending Story: Historical Developments in Canadian Archaeology and the Quest for Federal Heritage Legislation. *Canadian Journal of Archaeology* 18, 77–98.

Coleman, D. and R. Williamson (1994) Landscapes Past to Landscapes Future: Planning for Archaeological Resources. In R. MacDonald (ed.) *Great Lakes Archaeology and Paleoecology: Exploring Interdisciplinary Initiatives for the Nineties*, 61–80. Waterloo.

Ellis, Ch. and N. Ferris (eds) (1990) *The Archaeology of Southern Ontario to A.D. 1650*. (Occasional Publications of the London Chapter, Ontario Archaeological Society, Number 5). London/Ontario.

Ferris, N. (1988) *Subdivision Survey and Reporting Guidelines: Questionnaire Responses*. (Report for the 1988 Meeting on Archaeological Technical Standards. Ontario Ministry of Culture & Communications). Toronto.

Ferris, N. (1998) 'I Don't Think We're in Kansas Anymore...': The Rise of the Archaeological Consulting Industry in Ontario. In P. Smith and D. Mitchell (eds) *Bringing Back the Past Historical Perspectives on Canadian Archaeology*, 225–247. (Archaeological Survey of Canada, Mercury Series, Paper 158). Ottawa.

Ferris, N. (1999) What's in a Name? The Implications of Archaeological Terminology Used in Non-archaeological Contexts. In R. Williamson and Ch. Watts (eds) *Taming the Taxonomy Towards a New Understanding of Great Lakes Archaeology*, 111–121. Toronto.

Ferris, N. (2000) Current Issues in the Governance of Archaeology in Canada. *Canadian Journal of Archaeology* 24 (2), 164–170.

Ferris, N. (2002) Where the Air Thins: The Rapid Rise of the Archaeological Consulting Industry in Ontario. *Revista de Arqueología Americana* 21, 53–88.

Ferris, N. (2003) Between Colonial and Indigenous Archaeologies: Legal and Extra-Legal Ownership of the Archaeological Past in North America. *Canadian Journal of Archaeology* 27,154–190.
Ferris, N. (2004) Guess Who Sat Down to Dinner? Archaeology in Laws. In W. Lovis (ed.) *An Upper Great Lakes Archaeological Odyssey: Essays in Honor of Charles E. Cleland*, 199–214. Detroit.
Fowler, J. (1995) The Legal Structure for the Protection of Archaeological Resources in the United States and Canada. In R. Knudson and B. Keel (eds) *The Public Trust and the First Americans*, 75–86. Corvallis.
Fox, W. (1982) The Calvert Village: Glen Meyer Community Patterns. *Kewa* 82 (7–8), 5–9.
Fox, W. (1990) *Heritage Conservation and Development Plans Review*. Toronto.
Green, W. and Doershuk, J. (1998) Cultural Resource Management and American Archaeology. *Journal of Archaeological Research* 6 (2), 121–167.
MacLeod, D. (1977) Peddle or Perish: Archaeological Marketing From Concept to Product Delivery. In M. Schiffer and G. Gumerman (eds) *Conservation Archaeology A Guide for Cultural Resource Management Studies*, 63–72. New York.
Noble, W. (1982) Potsherds, Potlids and Politics: An Overview of Ontario Archaeology during the 1970's. *Canadian Journal of Archaeology* 6, 167–194.
Ogilvie, R. (1990) *Report On Heritage Conservation (Specifically Archaeology) In Municipal Planning*. (Report of Ogilvie, Ogilvie and Company for the Ontario Ministry of Culture). Toronto.
Ontario Ministry of Culture (1993) *Cultural Heritage Resource Conservation Within the Land Use Planning Process in the Province Of Ontario: Archaeological Assessment Technical Guidelines – Stage 1–3 Assessment and Reporting*. Toronto.
Ontario Ministry of Culture (1997) *Conserving a Future for our Past: Archaeology, Land Use Planning and Development in Ontario. An Educational Primer and Comprehensive Guide for Non-Specialists*. Toronto.
Parker, L. (1996) Letter to the Editor. *Arch Notes,* (N.S. 1–3), 18–19.
Smith, L. (2004) *Archaeological Theory and the Politics of Cultural Heritage*. Oxfordshire.
Stewart, B. (1986) The Frontenac Village Site; Whose Responsibility? In W. Fox (ed.) *Archaeological Consulting in Ontario: Papers of the London Conference 1985*, 73–76. (Occasional Publications of the London Chapter, Ontario Archaeological Society, Number 2, 3–8). London/Ontario.
Timmins, P. (1997) *The Calvert Site an Interpretive Framework for the Early Iroquoian Village*. (Archaeological Survey of Canada, Mercury Series, Paper Number 156). Ottawa.
Turnbull, Ch. (1977) Of Backdirt and Bureaucracy: The Role of Government in Canadian Archaeology. In A. McKay (ed.) *New Perspectives in Canadian Archaeology*, 119–136. Ottawa.
Tyyska, A. (1986) Private Sector Involvement in Archaeology. In W. Fox (ed.) *Archaeological Consulting in Ontario: Papers of the London Conference 1985*, 3–8. (Occasional Publications of the London Chapter, Ontario Archaeological Society, Number 2, 3–8). London/Ontario.
Williamson, R. (2000) Trends and Issues in Consulting Archaeology. *Canadian Journal of Archaeology* 24 (2), 158–162.

CHAPTER 8

Quality management of archaeology in Great Britain: present practice and future challenges

Peter Hinton and David Jennings

ARCHAEOLOGY IN THE UNITED KINGDOM

During the 1980s it became increasingly common for developers in the United Kingdom to pay for the archaeological work that their schemes entailed, often as a condition for receiving permission to develop from a local government planning authority. This system became formalised in England in 1990 with the publication of Planning Policy Guidance note 16 Archaeology and Planning (Department of the Environment 1990), and then elsewhere in the UK though similar planning guidance, and is recognisable in some of the articles of the 'European Convention on the Protection of the Archaeological Heritage (Council of Europe 1992), more commonly known as the Valletta or Malta Convention.

Today, most archaeological work in the UK is developer funded (figure 8.1). Statistics are limited, but the most recent figures for England (1999/2000; Aitchison 2000) indicate that central government and EU funds contributed £ 19 million (*c.* € 27 million), local government £ 25 million (*c.* € 35 million) and developers £ 68 million (*c.* € 95 million). Estimates for 2003/4 suggest similar figures for central and local government, but an increase to £ 144 million (*c.* € 202 million) in developer spending (Kenneth Aitchison, pers. comm.).

Most of that developer funding is spent on investigating sites that are not formally designated. In England in April 2004 there were 19,594 scheduled monuments, 371,971 listed buildings, 584 registered parks and gardens, and 1,430,000 sites and monuments recorded on non-statutory Sites and Monuments Records (English Heritage 1994). In other words 98.7% of known archaeological sites are not scheduled. This ratio is echoed in the rest of the UK.

In England, Scotland and Wales there is no system of excavation licences. Excavation of a scheduled monument (that cherished 1.3%) requires scheduled monument consent, based on approval of project design; excavation of any unscheduled site or monument as part of redevelopment may require approval of a project design by a planning authority; but the general rule is that anyone has the right to excavate an archaeological site, providing they do not infringe the property rights of the owner of the land. In Northern Ireland licensing does exist: the remainder of this paper is therefore concerned only with Great Britain (England, Scotland and Wales), not the United Kingdom (of Great Britain and Northern Ireland).

Figure 8.1 In today's Britain, archaeology is very much part of the planning and construction world, with most excavations commissioned by private developers (Winchester Library Site, Photo Oxford Archaeology).

QUALITY MANAGEMENT IN DEVELOPER-FUNDED ARCHAEOLOGY

While we intend neither to undertake a linguistic analysis nor offer philosophical insight into our understanding of the word 'quality', it is worthwhile to begin our consideration with a few observations. First, as with many terms, we use it in a variety of senses as archaeologists operating in a developer-funded sector. Traditionally, given the academic roots of the discipline, we consider quality as the 'degree of excellence of a thing' (Oxford English Dictionary). In commercial circles, however, different definitions are applied such as 'conformance to specification', 'meeting customer requirements', 'satisfying the customer', 'fitness for use'; or, looking to ISO 9000 'the totality of features and characteristics of a product or service that bear on its ability to satisfy stated or implied needs'.

We offer the thought that confusion can arise as we slip between different meanings of quality and their associations. In particular, this can be seen in the context of the two main narratives that dominate professional archaeology: a 'curatorial' narrative that is concerned with the description, management and protection of the historic environment in the modern world; and a narrative of historical enquiry which seeks to make meaningful statements about the past. While these two narratives are clearly inter-related, it should be clear that most of our concerns with respect to quality in terms of historical enquiry revolve around issues highlighted in the Oxford English Dictionary's definition; meanwhile within a curatorial context, our thoughts often tend towards concerns over compliance with standards and specifications.

Naturally, the 'slipperiness' of language is well-rehearsed, but it is still of benefit to consider its beguiling aspects: too often faults in our thinking are caused by lack of adequate transparency.

We should recognise that reflections on 'quality' do necessarily pose questions regarding the purpose of our activities, and given the enormous diversity of approaches to archaeology within the discipline, it means that, to varying degrees, contention will remain at the heart of any discussion about the quality of work.

Against the background of these introductory comments in practice, quality management is seen as working in a tri-partite way; assessing and regulating the suitability of work by *process*, by *product* and by *person*. To be effective, attention is required to all three (figure 8.2). Explicit application of a three-part system of quality management to archaeology was fundamental to the proposals of the *Nederlandse Vereniging van Archeologen* (NVvA, the Dutch archaeologists' professional association; see for example Knoop 2001).

Typically in British developer-funded archaeology, a planning authority (or its archaeologist) will respond to a proposal to develop a site by setting an outline brief for the work that is required to assess or mitigate archaeological damage. The developer (or his/her archaeologist) then prepares a detailed project design for the planning authority to approve – or, of course, reject. Subject to approval the developer commissions the archaeological work and in due course submits his/her report, prepared by the archaeologist. The planning authority accepts the report – or sends it back. With the report published and archive deposited, or a binding agreement that this will happen, the 'planning condition' is discharged: the developer is released from his/her commitment and the archaeologist completes the project. Scheduled monument consent follows similar principles, though the process is presently managed by national heritage bodies on behalf of the state, not by local government.

It can be seen that this process of approving the project design and finished report is quality management by *process* and *product*, not by *person*: it addresses two corners of the triangle. By contrast, article 3 of the Valletta Convention states that 'To preserve the archaeological heritage and guarantee the scientific significance of archaeological research work each party undertakes:

i) to apply procedures for the authorisation and supervision of excavation and other archaeological activities in such a way as

- to prevent any illicit damage or removal of elements of the archaeological heritage

Figure 8.2 The scale and pace of archaeological projects requires close adherence to standards and a focus on quality if we are to preserve accurate records to enable future research (Northgate House, Winchester, Photo Oxford Archaeoloy).

- to ensure that excavations and prospecting are undertaken in a scientific manner

ii) to ensure that excavations and other potentially destructive techniques are carried out only by qualified, specially authorised *persons*' (Council of Europe 1992).'

This is quality management by *person*, not by *process* and *product*, addressing only the corner of the triangle ignored in Britain. The Valletta Convention was ratified by the UK government on 21 September 2000 and – in theory – was implemented on 21 March 2001.

Therefore, with reference to our earlier comments, it is apparent that quality in the sense of 'conformance to specification' and related definitions, which tend to dominate in the curatorial narrative, are relatively well supported in terms of process and product. The absence of quality management by person leads to a larger degree of anxiety in relation to the 'quality of knowledge about the past', if we are allowed to use such a short-hand with all of the accepted caveats.

THE INSTITUTE OF FIELD ARCHAEOLOGISTS

The Institute of Field Archaeologists (IFA) is the professional association for archaeologists in the UK, but is increasingly attracting members from continental Europe (mid July 2006, the total number of archaeologists in Great Britain was 2176; the number of IFA-members was 2223; the number of IFA-members from Europe was 28; and the number of IFA-members from the rest of the world was 19). Its mission statement reads 'We advance the practice of archaeology and allied disciplines by promoting professional standards and ethics for conserving, managing, understanding and promoting enjoyment of the heritage' – encompassing the curatorial and historical enquiry narratives.

Fundamental to the IFA is its code of conduct (IFA 2002; IFA 2006; www.archaeologists.net/modules/icontent/index.php?page=15) which sets out the ethical conduct expected of all IFA members. The IFA seeks to ensure compliance by addressing all three corners of the quality management triangle.

Quality management by person

There are several grades of individual membership of the IFA:

- Affiliate: interested in archaeology
- Student: studying archaeology
- Practitioner (PIFA): doing archaeological work
- Associate (AIFA): exercising responsibility for archaeological work
- Member (MIFA): exercising substantial responsibility for archaeological work

Members are admitted to the three 'corporate' grades of PIFA, AIFA and MIFA through rigorous scrutiny of their qualifications, career, work and personal references: they undertake to abide by the code of conduct, other by laws and supporting documents.

Registered archaeological organisations (RAO's) undertake, as organisations, to operate according to the code of conduct, by-laws and standards and guidance. They are led by an archaeologist with the highest grade of IFA membership. Unlike individual members, they re-apply for registration every two years, and are monitored and inspected by the IFA.

Quality management by process and product

The IFA has devised standards and guidance for desk-based assessments, field evaluation, excavation, watching briefs, building investigation and recording and finds work (www.archaeologists.net/modules/icontent/index.php?page=15); hard copy of the code of conduct, all the standards and guidance and other constitutional documents are available from the IFA); and is preparing further standards for *stewardship* (conservation and management of the historic environment), nautical archaeology recording and reconstruction, and survey. These documents contain two elements. The first is the Standard, which sets out what a piece of work must achieve (*e.g.* "an archaeological excavation will examine and record the nature of the archaeological resource within a specified area using appropriate methods and practices. It will result in one of more published accounts and an ordered, accessible archive"). The standard defines what the *product* must lead to. A much longer section is devoted to Guidance on how the standard can be met, on *processes* that should normally be followed and a more detailed description of the elements of the report *produced*. The guidance is not extremely detailed, as archaeologists should be free to innovate and adapt; and they may even depart from the guidance providing that, if challenged, they can demonstrate good reason – consistent with the code of conduct – for doing so.

Complaints and discipline

IFA members agree to be subject to the Institute's disciplinary procedures should the IFA learn of potential infractions of the code of conduct or receive a formal allegation of misconduct. Similarly, a thorough procedure governs complaints about RAO's. The procedures for individuals and RAO's are different, but in summary outcomes of investigations can result in dismissal of the allegation ('no case to answer'), an advisory recommendation (*e.g.* doing a piece of work again, making a financial compensation, apologising, retraining), a formal reprimand, suspension from membership or expulsion.

Investigation and enforcement are taken seriously. In 2005 six members were the subject of disciplinary investigations or proceedings: one received a written warning as to future conduct, two were the subject of advisory recommendations and three are still subject to disciplinary investigation or process. In the same year four registered organisations were investigated, resulting in a range of responses: additionally an organisation was removed from the register when it became clear that it had supplied false information in support of its application for registration.

BARRIERS TO ENTRY TO COMMERCIAL PRACTICE

What happens when archaeologists or organisations are thrown out of the IFA? Professional embarrassment, definitely. Reduced opportunities to get a job or win work, certainly – up to a point. But at present there are no restrictions on who can practise archaeology in Great Britain. The national heritage bodies have made a commitment to compliance with the Valletta convention. They will, where appropriate, require accredited archaeologists for work on scheduled monuments and work they fund, but the timescale for implementation is unclear – March 2001 is long past. The intention is that the national heritage bodies should use their influence with local and national government to ensure that similar procedures are applied in local government, which, as stated above, oversees the vast majority of archaeological work in Great Britain.

In the absence of effective barriers to entry to professional practice, it is hard for the IFA to drive forward improvements in archaeological quality as fast as it would like. Life may be harder but it is certainly not impossible for those that find it too expensive, uncompetitive or inconvenient to improve in order to maintain their membership or registration with the institute. And in Britain, as elsewhere, there are archaeologists who see no reason to maintain their education or to change the practices they were comfortable with ten or twenty years ago – "but we've always done it this way".

It is not only the lack of 'regulatory muscle' for the IFA resulting from the indifferent application of the Valletta Convention that compromises quality. The absence of barriers to entry has a profound effect on the economics of the archaeological market, leading to low profitability, which in turn reduces the capacity of contracting organisations to invest in training, research and design and Continual Professional Development (CPD). Michael Porter's Five Forces Model still provides one of the most powerful demonstrations of this point (Porter 1980), as it provides a framework for understanding industry structure and levels of profitability. In essence Porter outlines that in order to understand the structure of an industry you have to consider the five forces of suppliers, substitutes, buyers, new entrants and industry rivalry (figure 8.3). Taking these in turn, we would offer the following observations.

Suppliers and substitutes

In general, within the sector the power of suppliers is a relatively modest factor. There are not significant single-suppliers that exercise considerable control over the capacity of archaeological organisations to compete, as most costs relate to staff rather than materials. In sectors where suppliers do exercise considerable power, competitive advantage can be derived from close supply chain management. For archaeology, however, supply chain control is of relatively limited significance in terms of our competitive strategy, and has therefore limited impact on organisational effectiveness.

At first sight it might appear that there is only a very restricted number of substitutes that might impact upon the archaeological market. For the core operation of excavation and related services this is correct. Around the periphery, however, there is a slightly wider range of substitute providers from cemetery clearance companies for burials, through to conservation architects for building recording and non-specialised multi-disciplinary consultancies that provide heritage advice. Even with these provisos it is apparent that the power of substitutes is only moderate within the sector.

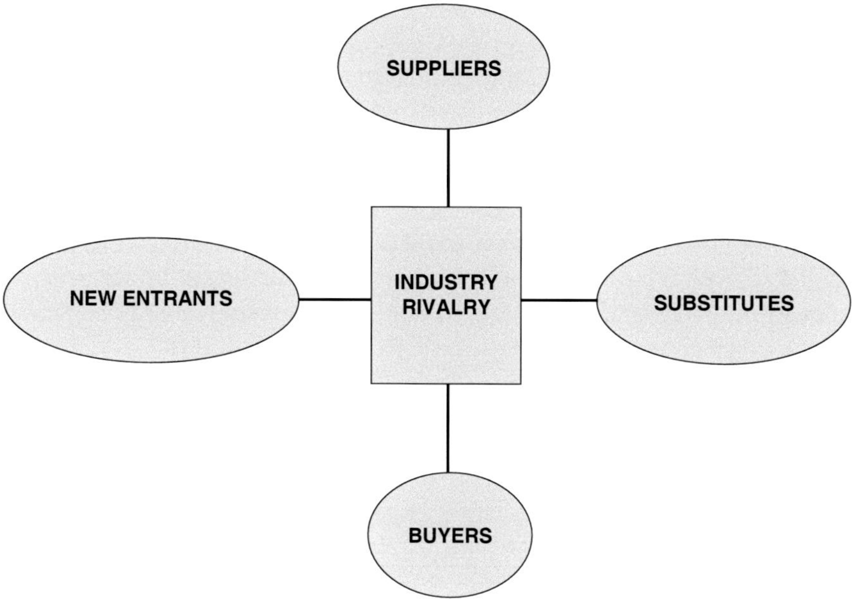

Figure 8.3 Porter's Five Forces Model.

Buyers and new entrants

It is obvious that if suppliers and substitutes do little to shape the competitive environment, the power of buyers has a very significant impact. This truism is really so widely accepted that it does not really require elaboration. When buyer power is considered in conjunction with the ease with which new companies can enter the archaeological market, we can begin to appreciate the factors that shape the archaeological market in Great Britain and define the levels of current industry rivalry.

The key elements of buyers' strengths that we might want to pull out are:

- the archaeological products/services that are purchased are relatively standard and undifferentiated;
- buyers face few costs in switching from one supplier to another;
- buyers earn low profits (while many archaeologists believe that developers are 'rapacious entities rolling in money', this is very far from the truth – the stock market is a very hard taskmaster for many archaeologists' clients with an emphasis on short-term profits and maximum returns);
- the archaeological product/service is normally perceived as unimportant to the quality of the buyers' products or services (for all that we argue that heritage-led design reflecting the history of the site can add value to commercial or residential properties);

- the buyer has full information – this was not always so, but the rise of intermediate archaeological consultancies offering advice to developers in the procurement and operation of archaeological contractors means that buyers are now far better informed: in classical economics it is seen that this tends to drive prices down.

As stated above, it is a reality that the barriers to entry are frighteningly low for our sector, given that you do not need to be registered or chartered to operate as an archaeologist. These low entry barriers increase the strength of buyer power as there is almost no constriction on the number of archaeological service providers, resulting in a fragmented industry (see industry rivalry below).

Industry rivalry

Stated bluntly, the archaeological market in Great Britain can be characterised by a high degree of fragmentation, poor/restricted profitability (less than 5%), uneven regulation, low barriers to entry and increasing competition. That competition, despite all of the assertions of every single archaeological practice to offer a high quality service, is highly price sensitive given the power of buyers outlined above.

In terms of fragmentation, one author's recent rapid assessment of competitors revealed that 100 competitors in the archaeological market in England could be easily identified, and this was by no means an exhaustive analysis. Also, it is significant to note that even market leaders with turnovers in the order of £ 6–8 million could only claim to have approximately 5% of the market, and therefore do not have the capacity to set market prices or influence them to any significant degree.

Profitability

Having established the structure of the industry, Porter then looks at the impact entry and exit barriers have on industry profitability (figure 8.4). We might consider that archaeology ought to be positioned in the 'low stable returns' box. However, we would contend that there are factors in the market that tend to push it closer to the 'low risky returns' arena. While archaeology's exit barriers are not of the scale of those in industries like steel and chemical production, there are, nevertheless, very powerful vocational drivers that keep organisations in the sector even when the work is barely profitable. Equally, an argument can be developed that a broad number of the organisations that operate in the archaeological market do not face the complete economic reality of the market. For instance, organisations based in local authorities and universities do not have to pay attention to cash flow, as their cash requirements are absorbed by being part of a much larger entity. Given that most bankrupted businesses are profitable but simply run out of cash, this is a significant factor. It can be argued on occasion that these organisations may not be paying the real cost for services, or their lack of profitable performance might be tolerated for

Exit Barriers

		LOW	HIGH
Entry barriers	LOW	Low stable returns	Low risky returns
	HIGH	High stable returns	High risky returns

Figure 8.4 Entry and exit barriers and profitability.

other 'political' reasons – or that the complexities of accounting procedures in some larger organisations make it difficult to accurately account for the performance of their archaeological arms. Equally many archaeological organisations that are part of these larger entities have to face disproportionately burdensome overhead charges, and other factors that make it difficult for them to compete.

On another front, the support and rescue packages that have been offered in the past to organisations that have got into financial difficulties (from a very legitimate concern for the archaeological archives) means that market forces are not permitted to operate. As a consequence, it can be argued that prices are being driven to artificially low levels – to the point where there is sensitivity concerning quality in all of its aspects.

We have taken the opportunity to present a view of the sector from within the model presented by Porter, as it offers insight into some of the recurrent debate that revolves around the concerns over standards. Critics of the IFA and managers of archaeological organisations question why the Institute cannot impose stringent standards far in excess of current practice, or why contracting organisations do not simply agree to charge more for work to create a more profitable structure for the industry. Porter emphasises that just as is the case with individuals, the IFA and organisations do not have full control of the situation. Indeed in relation to the five forces, at best we only constitute the whole of one force. The external pressures are such that with the current barriers to entry and exit, we *cannot* engineer a strategy within our core business that will lead to high stable profits. To achieve that objective there needs to be some adjustment to our operating environment and this needs to be driven around a raising of the barriers to entry.

Indeed, the realities of the current market suggest that we might make this statement more forcefully. At present in Great Britain's archaeology market it is apparent that with low entry barriers and heightened exit barriers, the market is becoming increasingly saturated with service providers. Given the buyer power discussed above, this is resulting in a downward pressure on prices which in classical economics reduces profitability to the bottom limits of tolerance. According to orthodoxy, in a saturated market we should expect higher levels of bankruptcy as the 'inefficient' are driven out of the market. This presents real concerns to the sector, in relation to ongoing practice and the retention of appropriate standards, as organisations come under increasing pressure. From this perspective, however, it might be argued (possibly at first sight counter-intuitively) that we need to allow the market to work, in order for the market-place to find an appropriate level. It is obvious that at this time, more than ever before, we also need effective regulation to ensure that the survival of an organisation is not at the expense of the archaeological record.

STATE-RECOGNISED ACCREDITATION OF ARCHAEOLOGISTS – THE WAY FORWARD?

The IFA and the Institute of Historic Building Conservation (IHBC) have recently proposed – initially to English Heritage, which is leading discussions on behalf of Historic Scotland and Cadw (Wales), a combined accreditation framework for historic environment professionals. For archaeological organisations we propose that the RAO scheme is adequate, but for individuals accreditation would need to assess not only their competence and commitment to ethics at the point of entry, but would also have to cover a limited period of time and require a commitment to CPD. The distinction is made because the IFA recognises that quality assurance of registered organisations is more reliable than it is for individual members: for RAO's the IFA looks more closely at their work, it does so every two years (whereas members are assessed only at entry, if they seek to upgrade their membership or if it appears that there may have been misconduct), and it carries out office (figure 8.5) and site inspections. Critically, CPD is not yet compulsory for individual members.

So the IFA and IHBC need to continue to develop a suite of standards and guidance to reflect all types of historic environment work, to put in place the full range of mechanisms for quality management by *process* and *product*. This is in hand, but may never end. Additionally, they need to introduce a system of quality management by *person* that is as effective for individuals as it is for companies or government bodies. This will mean being prepared to accept that there are faults in the current approach, and that significant change is required.

British heritage agencies must be prepared to participate in the development of a reformed accreditation framework. They need to accept that accreditation must be linked to subscription to the disciplinary procedures of the IFA and IHBC, as

Figure 8.5 Inspection is an important part of becoming a Registered Archaeological Organisation, and involves critical but constructive discussion of an organisation's practices (Photo Alison Taylor, IFA).

there must be a system of sanctions against transgressors. The heritage agencies must also require accredited archaeologists for most scheduled monument consents and work they pay for, and they must encourage planning authorities to do likewise. Importantly – and in some ways this may be a treasured peculiarity of UK archaeology – there must be sufficient flexibility in the accreditation system and its application by authorities to ensure that the amateur or voluntary sector is encouraged to participate in all aspects of archaeological work. The IFA wishes to promote professional standards to all archaeologists, paid and unpaid, not to reduce public involvement and interest in the discipline it so passionately believes in.

CONCLUSIONS

This paper has principally focussed on the role of the IFA in the sphere of quality management. We have argued that while archaeology in Great Britain operates relatively successfully with respect to the regulation of process and product, it still needs to develop robust procedures for individual regulation. We have broadened our assessment to argue that the lack of entry barriers resulting from a failure to implement Article 3 of the Valletta Convention is compromising the sector's capacity to drive forward standards and inward investment. Given the increasing saturation of the archaeological market, we consider that pressure on standards is likely to increase as organisations come under increasing pressure to compete on the basis of price.

Despite the occasionally sombre tone of aspects of this paper, it should not be concluded that the introduction of the market-place into British archaeology has led to a reduction in the quality of archaeology. Indeed, we would rather state that the quality of archaeological recording, and curatorial provision has increased exponentially over the past 16 years – at least in part resulting from a concentration on quality management and a desire for effective self-regulation that scarcely existed before the competitive era arrived. We are now, however, faced with the challenges of an evolving market and an incipient profession. Conviction and determination of purpose are now required to ensure that working together the archaeological community can lead the sector to a stage of stable maturity.

ACKNOWLEDGEMENTS

The authors would like to thank Willem Willems and Monique van den Dries for inviting Peter Hinton to give a version of part of this paper to the September 2005 meeting of the European Association of Archaeologists in Cork, Eire; and to Adrian Olivier and Katalin Wollák for inviting both of us to give papers, combined in this document, to the October 2005 meeting of Europae Archaeologicae Consilium in Roses, Spain.

Above all, thanks should go to all those members of the Institute of Field Archaeologists who have helped evolve the UK's present system of archaeological quality management through self-regulation. For advice on accreditation, we are grateful to Seán O'Reilly (Institute of Historic Building Conservation), Prof. Andy Friedman (Professional Associations Research Network), and Sue Cole and Adrian Olivier (English Heritage).

References

Aitchison, K. (2000) The funding of professional archaeological practice in England. *Cultural Trends* 39, 1–32.

Council of Europe (1992) *European convention on the protection of the archaeological heritage (revised).* Brussels.

Department of the Environment (1990) *Planning Policy Guidance note 16. Archaeology and Planning.* London.

English Heritage (1994) *Heritage Counts.* London.

Institute of Field Archaeologists (2002) *Code of conduct.* Reading.

Institute of Field Archaeologists (2006) *Institute of Field Archaeologists Yearbook and Directory 2006.* Tisbury.

Jacobs, E. (ed.) (2001) *Derde nationale congres Nederlandse Vereniging van Archeologen.* Amsterdam.

Knoop, R. R. (2001) Een terugblik op de afgelopen jaren. In E. Jacobs (ed.) *Derde nationale congres Nederlandse Vereniging van Archeologen*, 15–24. Amsterdam.

Porter M. E. (1980) *Competitive strategy: techniques for analysing industries and competitors.* New York.

CHAPTER 9

Cultural resource management guidelines and practice in the United States

Evan Peacock and Janet Rafferty

INTRODUCTION

Compliance-driven archaeology (a part of cultural resource management, or CRM) began in the United States with passage of the Antiquities Act of 1906. Work associated with government-funded land development increased in scope and intensity with Depression-era federal relief programs in the 1930s and 1940s (Lyon 1996) and with the passage of further laws such as the Reservoir Salvage Act of 1960. With passage of the National Historic Preservation Act (NHPA) in 1966, the number of CRM projects and practitioners increased dramatically. Today there are thousands of CRM archaeologists in the US working for firms or as specialists in state or federal agencies.

This growth has had both beneficial and detrimental consequences. Obviously, a great deal of archaeology gets done, often in areas or at sites that might otherwise never be investigated. CRM has provided enormous amounts of data on the entire prehistoric and historic sequence of occupation in North America. And, of course, many opportunities now exist for those who seek to do archaeology as a profession. But there also are many problems with the way archaeology is done within a resource management framework. It is not only convenient but accurate to discuss these problems in terms of quality assurance, or QA. In this chapter, we review some of the main areas in which QA should be a major concern for American archaeologists, explore the reasons why it is sometimes compromised, and briefly discuss options for addressing the problems raised.

THE BASIC FRAMEWORK

The CRM process in the US has recently been described in detail by Hutt *et al.* (1992), King (2004, 2005), Neumann and Sanford (2001), and others. In brief, any undertaking on federal or tribal lands, or any undertaking on private lands that involves the use of federal funds or a permit, requires consideration of cultural resources, including archaeological remains. This usually unfolds in a three-part process: phase I survey (locating and preliminary evaluation of sites), phase II testing (excavation or other work designed to determine whether a given site is eligible for listing on the National Register of Historic Places), and phase III mitigation (usually full-scale excavation) if an eligible site cannot be avoided. State and local laws may also have to be contended with. QA issues arising from this process can be discussed under the following headings: qualifications, research designs, field and laboratory methods, significance determinations, report review, and enforcement.

QUALIFICATIONS

Who is qualified to do archaeology for pay in the US? State and federal agencies have generally adopted the US Secretary of Interior's guidelines, according to which the professional qualifications for a supervisory-level professional are a master's degree in archaeology, anthropology, or "closely related field", plus:

1. At least one year of full-time professional experience or equivalent specialized training in archeological research, administration or management;
2. At least four months of supervised field and analytic experience in general North American archeology; and
3. Demonstrated ability to carry research to completion.

> 'In addition to these minimum qualifications, a professional in prehistoric archeology shall have at least one year of full-time professional experience at a supervisory level in the study of archeological resources of the prehistoric period. A professional in historic archeology shall have at least one year of full-time professional experience at a supervisory level in the study of archeological resources of the historic period' (Code of Federal Regulations, 36 CFR Part 61).

These standards define the "minimum education and experience required" for the "identification, evaluation, registration, and treatment" of archaeological resources. Thus, the wording almost universally referenced, paraphrased or copied into state and federal regulations and policy manuals unequivocally states that, in order to identify and deal with archaeological remains, a graduate degree plus considerable experience in the field and lab is *required*. It is a violation of federal regulations to have field crews operating without a master's-level professional there to insure proper "identification, evaluation", and so on. But what happens on the ground is often a different reality altogether, as a few examples will suffice to illustrate.

According to Section 106 of the NHPA, all federal agencies – the Park Service, the Forest Service, the Bureau of Land Management, the Natural Resources Conservation Service, the Fish and Wildlife Service, etc. – must "take into account" the effects of their undertakings on archaeological resources. Practically, this amounts to doing archaeological survey in proposed impact zones, whether that impact is to be from logging, reservoir construction, or some other undertaking. To accomplish this work, agencies have staff archaeologists and/or let contracts to CRM firms. But other situations also exist. On some national forests, for example, surveys are routinely carried out by 'Heritage Resource Technicians', agency personnel who have attended a one-week training session in archaeology. Graduate students can enhance their education by interning with Forest Service archaeologists, but this often results in the students doing unsupervised fieldwork. The Natural Resources Conservation Service enables a vast number of ground-moving projects each year, the majority of which clearly qualify as "undertakings" (US Natural Resources Conservation Service General Manual Title 420, Part 401.3). They do not maintain a professional archaeological staff large enough to inspect that many project areas. Instead, they have a training program in which their other field staff are exposed to some of the basics of archaeology and then required to report to the agency archaeologist if they see anything noteworthy. Such examples represent apparent violations of the standards to which the agencies subscribe.

The pressure for such structures to evolve is enormous, given the daunting tasks faced by cash-strapped federal agencies trying to manage a non-renewable resource that is likely to be present in many, if not most, proposed project areas. The argument is that technicians can be trained to locate sites while the critical part of the process – evaluating those sites for significance – can subsequently be accomplished by agency archaeologists as time allows. Whatever legal standing this argument has comes through Programmatic Agreements, Memoranda of Understanding, and Memoranda of Agreement crafted by the agencies and ultimately signed by them, the Advisory Council on Historic Preservation (an independent federal agency reporting directly to the President), and State Historic Preservation Officers, or SHPO's (*e.g.* US Natural Resources Conservation Service and Others 2002). Such agreements help streamline the Section 106 process by, for example, defining minimally destructive undertakings that can be exempted from the process as 'categorical exclusions'. Left implicit in many of them, however, is who will actually identify archaeological remains in the field when surveys are required. In others, technicians and/or interns are explicitly allowed to conduct surveys without direct, in-the-field supervision in specific circumstances (*e.g.* in small project areas) and even to make significance evaluations (*e.g.* US Forest Service and Others 1996).

While educating the rank and file of an agency about archaeology is commendable, using those personnel as the front line of resource identification surely leads, at a minimum, to a bias towards large, artifact-rich sites (*cf.* the exchange between Tainter 1979 and Fisher 1980 and the discussion in Reed 1987). The full detrimental effects of such practices remain unknown.

Harder to understand as regards qualifications is why agency archaeologists themselves often do not meet the criteria specified in the Secretary of Interior's guidelines. The US Forest Service, for example, has many archaeologists who do not hold graduate degrees. This may partly be a result of competition in the job market, but it also arguably is due to the misapplication of affirmative action and/or veterans preference policies. The agency – and indeed, all federal agencies – has a loophole in that the standards for a professional archaeologist outlined by the US Office of Personnel Management (OPM) are lower than those specified by the

Secretary of the Interior (King 2004, 332–334), despite the OPM's own assessment of the difficulties of the job:

> "Archeological problems are of such complexity and so unique that the intensity, advance [sic] nature, and breadth of knowledge required in their solution can be readily demonstrated as requiring qualifications *beyond the capacity of specialized technicians*. Assignments require the exercise of initiative, judgement, and resourcefulness to reconcile inadequate and conflicting data to a degree which requires the application of professional knowledge of and insight into physical phenomena and relationships in recognizing and defining problems and evaluating methods for their solution. The requirement for application of professional knowledge may also be based on the need for developing new solutions to archaeological problems". (US Office of Personnel Management 1983, 2; emphasis added).

One reason for requiring a thesis in most master's programs is to demonstrate just the kind of skills the OPM ostensibly is looking for in federal archaeologists, yet the system allows for hiring people at the "full performance levels" (GS-9 and above) who have not completed a master's degree. This practice is especially problematic where the hardest part of an archaeologist's job, significance evaluations, is concerned (*cf.* Moratto and Kelly 1978; Tainter and Lucas 1983). It also leads to the peculiar situation where contractors working on federal land have more stringent qualification requirements than the agency specialists who prepare the scopes of work and review the reports.

But what about commercial firms and independent consultants? Typically, when a client identifies a job that requires Section 106 review, the SHPO is contacted for a list of archaeological consultants. Although states usually make reference to the Secretary of Interior's guidelines, enforcement of those standards may be lacking where qualifications are concerned. Indeed, many SHPO's explicitly disavow any responsibility for insuring that qualifications are met. The North Carolina Office of State Archaeology, for example, states that "The [S]HPO assumes no responsibility for the accuracy of this [consultant] list and does not attest to the personal or corporate qualifications of persons or firms appearing herein" (http://www.arch.dcr.state.nc.us/ncarch/resource/consultants.html). Similarly, the Alabama Historical Commission provides a list of "individuals who have identified themselves [...] as Archaeologists" and states that "The [...] Commission makes no representation of the quality of the service to be performed by any individual on this list. All information on this list was provided by these individuals and has not been verified by the Alabama Historical Commission" (http://www.preserveala.org/ahcarchaeologistlist.html). In other words, 'let the buyer beware'. In the absence of state or federal enforcement, the client takes all the risk. If a report is rejected repeatedly by the SHPO's office, the client could refuse to pay the contractor. If substandard or fraudulent work is done, the client's only recourse is litigation against the consultant, a step that most will be unlikely to take. As a construction contractor once remarked to the senior author, "we'd just be throwing good money after bad".

Where both private consultants and agency archaeologists are concerned, compromising on government-specified qualifications is possibly one of the most serious QA problems in US archaeology. It certainly is one of the most egregious.

RESEARCH DESIGNS

In response to client requests, archaeologists in the US submit proposals for commercial work that include problem-oriented research designs. This practice evolved alongside the New Archaeology of the 1960s and 1970s (*e.g.* Binford 1964; Lipe 1978; Raab and Klinger 1977, 1979; Schiffer and Gumerman 1977; *cf.* Altschul 2005; Smith 2005; Tainter and Bagley 2005, 58) and resulted in many CRM monographs that were landmarks in American archaeology (*e.g.* McGimsey and Davis 1977; Schiffer and House 1975, 1977). As Dunnell (1984) has argued, however, the practice introduces systematic bias, as sites chosen and materials recovered using contemporary research designs may have little bearing on future archaeological questions (*cf.* Dixon 1977; Lipe 1974; Lynott 1980; McManamon 1977; McMillan *et al.* 1977; Peacock 1994, 1996; Raab and Klinger 1979; Raffino 1977; Sharrock and Grayson 1979; Smith 2005; Tainter 1987; Tainter and Lucas 1983).

This problem becomes especially pronounced when archaeologists fall into the trap of investigating their own conceptual units: *e.g.* when research is framed in terms of 'phases', which are archaeological constructs and not phenomenological entities. Phases, as used by American archaeologists, are ostensibly classes into which phenomena at the scale of occupation can be placed (Willey and Phillips 2001), rather than, for example, a specific period of building construction, as the term might be used in Europe. Though phases are supposed to be classes, they are, in fact, constructed in a *post facto* manner based upon observations made about the archaeological record. The pitfalls of such an approach are obvious, if mostly ignored: change the traits chosen for observation and the temporal and spatial boundaries of any such construct will change accordingly. As inductive units, phases also are historically contingent in that they are devised where people happened to have first looked. The traits – *e.g.* pottery types – are usually the result of inductive sorting rather than being types consciously constructed to address a particular problem. Choosing one such subjective trait (or groups of traits) and privileging its temporal and spatial distribution over any other also typically is done without theoretical justification (*cf.* Mathers, Schelberg and Kneebone 2005; Tainter and Bagley 2005). Typological thinking, which both derives from and promotes a normative, essentialist epistemology, is rampant within the discipline (*cf.* Mathers, Darvill and Little 2005, 9) and frequently becomes codified when states require that archaeologists "use existing typologies" to describe and/or interpret materials recovered in CRM projects, even when such traditional types are not comparable in terms of the criteria used to construct them (Rafferty 1986). Why such inductively-derived constructs should be appropriate for organizing data in time and space in all situations is a question that is stubbornly avoided, even in the face of explicit theoretical challenges (*e.g.* Dunnell 1982; Fox 1998; Lipo *et al.* 1997; Lyman *et al.* 1997; O'Brien and Lyman 2003; Tainter and Bagley 2005; Wettstaed 2002; Wood 2002).

The use of components (the manifestation of a phase at a site) also can be misleading, as 'multi-component' sites are treated as though separate phenomenological entities are present when in fact a single occupation can exist over the period of time that the diagnostic artifacts were produced (Rafferty 2001). In other words, the divisions are arbitrary, not real, but they are treated as though they were real. Another problem is the rote categorization of sites at the phase I level (*e.g.* 'lithic scatter', 'base camp', 'house site'), an *a priori* assumption of function and relative importance that often results in prehistoric and historic archaeological phenomena being treated as redundant (see discussions by Butler 1987; Hardesty and Little 2000, 66–71; Glassow 1977; Mathers, Schelberg and Kneebone 2005, 170–171; McManamon 1990; Peacock and Patrick 1997; Scott 1990; Scovill *et al.* 1972; Tainter 1979; Tainter and Bagley 2005; Wilson 1990) when in fact variability is being masked by the categories used.

The yearning for a universal language in archaeology is understandable, especially for those at the state level tasked with reviewing reports. The result, however, is all too often a stultifying sameness in which archaeologists basically wind up demonstrating what has already been assumed. This is particularly the case in CRM due to time pressures. Arguably, most of what we learn from CRM these days comes through sheer serendipity: if we happen to come across something unexpected, it can be described and subsequently referred to should someone unearth a similar phenomenon elsewhere. In other words, knowledge generated by contemporary CRM is more likely to be inductively, rather than deductively generated (*cf.* Meighan 1986). Inductive knowledge can be extremely important, and indeed it is particularly important in CRM, where archaeologists can generate massive amounts of data that may not directly pertain to the goals outlined in their research designs (Schaafsma 1989). Still, the rationale behind requiring research designs was to promote a deductive approach in commercial archaeology so that something more than a general procedure of rote description and happenstance discovery was achieved. Unless such a deductive approach includes critical thinking about how our analytical units are conceptualized, whether they are appropriate to the questions being asked, and whether we are systematically biasing what is preserved or investigated, however, it fails to deliver on its promise.

FIELD AND LABORATORY METHODS

Despite the usual requirement for research designs, there is a continuing debate over whether CRM is research (*e.g.* Briuer 1996; Briuer and Mathers 1996; Butler 1987; Dunnell 1984; Green 1983; King 2004, xv; Mathers, Darvill and Little 2005; Neumann

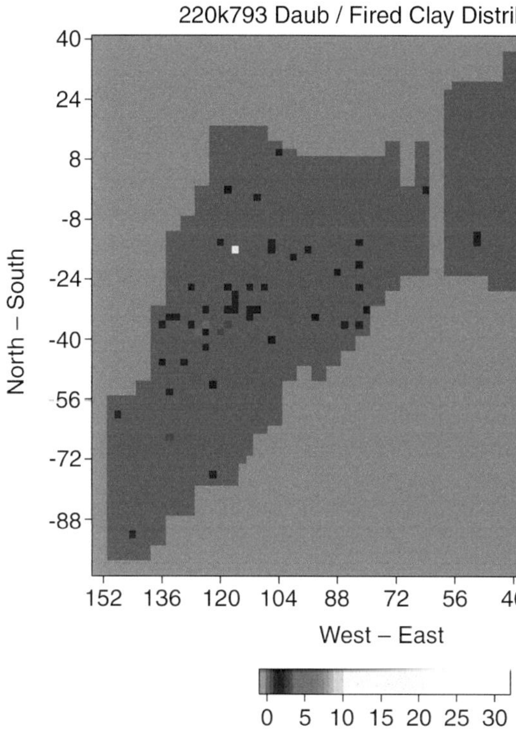

Figure 9.1 A controlled surface collection (CSC) map showing the distribution of daub on the surface of a site that was disked and collected in 2–meter square units. Two distinct concentrations mark the locations of two houses, one of which predated the other by a century or so. Had the site been stripped, these shallow remains would have been lost and the multiple occupations (Rafferty 2001) gone unrecorded.

and Sanford 2001, 12–13) in the true sense of the word. In CRM, sites in the way of development usually are evaluated for significance relative to other sites in the project area. Decisions about which sites to investigate ostensibly revolve around their potential to yield "information important in prehistory or history" (Code of Federal Regulations, 36 CFR 60.4, Criterion d), but with rare exceptions (*e.g.* Weaver *et al.* 1996) there is a clear bias toward large, artifact-rich sites with a relatively high likelihood of subsurface features. This bias is exemplified by the widespread use of site stripping at the phase II and phase III levels, often with no effort being made to assess the research value of surface artifact distributions beforehand (figure 9.1). Ironically, the use of geophysical equipment has tended to exacerbate this focus on features at the expense of other contexts. Geophysical survey is no magic bullet: for one thing, it can miss artifact concentrations and other kinds of features (*e.g.* Thacker *et al.* 2001), even when more than one kind of instrument is used. Thus, while geophysical survey is a complementary method for site investigation, it cannot simply replace more traditional field methods.

Those traditional methods have evolved over many decades and provide for the systematic recovery of artifacts from all contexts, if all contexts are given due consideration. Comparability is insured through standard requirements such as the use of quarter-inch screen and taking flotation samples from multiple contexts. The widespread acceptance and proven utility of such standard methods is one factor behind the argument that CRM is not research but a technical field, the practitioners of which are saving information that will be available and useful for future generations of researchers. Unfortunately, that utility is compromised when field methods are applied across the board in rote fashion, as is so often the case with stripping, for example. Another example is the continuing use of 10 cm excavation levels in almost all situations, even at sites with visible strata, causing artifacts from separate occupations to become mixed (*e.g.* Chapman *et al.* 1999; Connaway and McGahey 1971; Kuttruff *et al.* 1995).

If such problems are avoided and all contexts are adequately sampled, then materials retrieved via the methods of modern CRM will serve for addressing many research problems in the future. That is not to say that there is not room for improvement, of course. For one thing, more archaeologists need to recognize the potential for analyses that may be compromised by artifact processing procedures: *e.g.* the loss of residues when sherds or lithics are washed in the lab. Saving a sample of all kinds of artifacts in an unwashed state for long-term curation would be one way to start meeting such concerns. To give another example, it is only the fortuitous adherence of sediments to hominid teeth that has allowed ESR dating of remains excavated decades ago (*e.g.* Grün *et al.* 1991). While ESR is not likely to be much employed in American archaeology, sediment samples also allow for the measurement of background radiation levels needed for thermoluminescence dating. If collected and curated properly, sediment samples associated with archaeological remains doubtless will be useful in the future.

Another QA concern emerges in the analytical realm. As mentioned above, the potential for expanding our archaeological knowledge is greatly hampered when no deviations from traditional artifact typologies or space-time configurations are allowed. It is in the analysis stage that archaeologists have the chance to be at their most creative, to devise classifications that work to address specific problems rather than trying to use existing types or phases as omni-units appropriate for all kinds of enquiries. Stifling such creativity for bureaucratic convenience or traditionalist expectations surely is a disservice to the discipline and to the taxpaying public supporting CRM.

Figure 9.2 Mound A at the Poverty Point site, northeastern Louisiana. Large, visually impressive features such as earthen mounds are still the focus of much archaeological attention in the US.

SIGNIFICANCE DETERMINATIONS

All of the above-mentioned issues again come into consideration where significance determinations are concerned (*cf.* Altschul 2005; Darvill 2005; Tomlan 1998). The archaeological record of the US is vast and complex and, even if researchers' work is confined to a single region, they still will be confronted with enormous material variability. Many areas remain relatively unexplored, as evidenced by the fact that there are still counties with no recorded sites. Thus, the framework for interpretation and assessment is poorly developed in many parts of the country (*cf.* Glassow 1977; Plog 1981).

Site significance is determined based upon whether a site can be considered eligible for listing on the National Register of Historic Places (figure 9.2). As noted above, National Register Criterion d (36 CFR 60.4) states that a site can be considered eligible if it has "yielded, or may be likely to yield, information important in prehistory or history". As others have pointed out (*e.g.* Dixon 1977; Sharrock and Grayson 1979; Stuart and Gauthier 1981), this broad approach basically means that every site could be considered significant until proven otherwise. In fact, the process works the other way around, and archaeologists have to build cases for why particular sites should be considered significant. Ironically, one difficulty is that we know so little, especially about prehistory, that it can be hard to find detailed, specific reasons for asserting significance. The result is that determinations often reflect broad generalizations rather than precise questions (Altschul 2005, 197–198; Little 2005, 116): a site might be considered significant because it could yield information on 'subsistence during the Woodland period', for example, or on 'the transition to agriculture'. More commonly, significance has come to be equated with 'intact deposits', *i.e.* cultural strata or features below the plow zone.

While no one would argue that intact deposits are not important, the direct equation of the presence of such deposits with significance is problematic for two reasons. Firstly, there is a lack of consideration of what features and other 'intact' deposits actually represent. Features may contain fill that has nothing to do with original function, fill that has been redeposited, mechanically mixed, or bioturbated (*e.g.* Moeller 1992; Peacock *et al.* 2005). Yet features are perforce treated as though they represent temporally and functionally pristine archaeological events, and are therefore significant (figure 9.3). It is not uncommon to strip away unplowed midden to expose pits that are then excavated, even though those pits may be only holes in the subsoil containing remnant blobs of what was stripped away to expose them. Secondly, sites that apparently lack such 'intact deposits' may automatically be treated as being non-significant (*e.g.* Neumann and Sanford 2001, 33), an assumption that is not justified from a theoretical perspective. The argument from a management perspective is that sites with intact deposits will give more 'bang for the buck'. But suppose that a short-term, single-occupation site has been entirely plowed through. What might be learned from recovering the entire assemblage of artifacts from such a site, something that could be done rapidly and cheaply given that relatively little care would be needed for artifact recovery? Could not site function, raw material acquisition and use, seasonality, and other questions be addressed? The fact that many sites do not have intact deposits may well be an indication of their original nature rather than being wholly a result of post-depositional disturbance (*cf.* Butler 1987; Sullivan 1998; Tainter 1979). The truth is that we do not know what we are losing when such sites are automatically considered to be non-significant and consequently destroyed (Dancey 1998; Tainter and Bagley 2005). And if there are things we do not know, then there are things we can learn. Might not some of those things turn out to be "important in prehistory or history"?

REPORT REVIEW

CRM reports, which include determinations of site eligibility at the phase I and phase II levels, are sent to SHPO's for comment. Contrary to popular belief, an agency or client can disagree with a SHPO's assessment of site eligibility, recommendations for treatment of cultural remains, or other suggested courses of action. The SHPO's role is advisory once the Section 106 process has begun. Any agency or client that

Figure 9.3 A site being stripped in northern Mississippi. While stripping can be very useful, especially as a final step in salvage excavations, the privileging of features over other kinds of contexts has led to the rote use of stripping at earlier stages of investigation.

ignores the SHPO's advice opens itself up to scrutiny from outside parties, however, and the SHPO's word generally is treated as a mandate (Pickens 1998, 200–201). Disputes arising from the process can be referred to the Advisory Council on Historic Preservation, but this is a relatively rare occurrence: typically, only about 3% of disputed cases actually make it as far as the Advisory Council, with most being settled at the state level (Neumann and Sanford 2001, 38).

One of the most difficult tasks SHPO's have is reviewing reports to see if the archaeologists have complied with state guidelines and state and federal laws, to monitor the performance of individuals and firms over time, and to insure that proper permitting procedures are followed and the obligations thereof fulfilled. Also, fieldwork results are input into state-level databases (also known as the 'site files') for access and use by those involved in CRM.

This review step seems to provide the best opportunity for insuring QA in CRM in the US, and indeed, many problems are caught and dealt with at this stage. But state offices are perennially understaffed and underfunded, so that thorough review of all reports is usually unrealistic. Some states have employed an external peer-review system, which not only lightens the workload but also provides an objective opinion on the quality of work being performed. There is often little or no reward for reviewers, however, and it may be difficult to obtain outside reviews within the legally mandated 30–day comment period allotted SHPO's.

Another difficulty is that state employees tend to be poorly paid in relative terms, so that (*contra* Neumann and Sanford 2001, 11) it is unusual to have PhD-level professionals providing in-house reviews. Master's-level personnel are much more commonly employed, and it is not unknown to have people with Bachelor's degrees acting as Compliance Officers and reviewing reports. While such people may be as dedicated as any professional and may have considerable experience and skill, the degree to which they can act as QA backstops is debatable, especially if they are reviewing reports submitted by professionals with a higher academic standing. Attempts at innovation by CRM archaeologists may not be fully appreciated, and deviations from standard practice (*e.g.* employing a problem-oriented classification rather than a traditional typology) may actually be grounds for having a report rejected because such efforts will stand out from the mass of more traditional, descriptive reports. On more than one occasion, the authors have been asked by SHPO staff to insert into reports tables showing how problem-oriented artifact classes equate with traditional types, even though those traditional types are not suitable for the types of analysis being attempted. In the meantime, reports of questionable value (*e.g.* phase I reports with unexplained negative results) but cast in the traditional mold sail through the process unimpeded. A system that punishes innovation and rewards mediocrity clearly is a system in need of repair (*cf.* Altschul 2005).

ENFORCEMENT

There are areas other than qualifications where enforcement is lacking in US CRM. For example, while some federal agencies have made substantive efforts to survey all proposed impact zones, others have not achieved such a level of compliance. US Fish and Wildlife Service lands, for example, are divided into several regions. The Southeast Region arguably contains the richest, most complex body of archaeological remains in the country, with ca. 14,000 years of human occupation being represented in ten states, Puerto Rico, and the Virgin Islands. Yet the agency has *two* archaeologists for the entire region, who are expected to manage the cultural resources on over 1,250,000 hectares of land. It is patently impossible for two people (one of whom deals exclusively with paperwork and database management) to survey all areas where undertakings are proposed, or to manage contracts for that much area. The result is that only major projects receive adequate treatment under Section 106 while more everyday activities, such as logging, occur following procedural review but without surveys being done. This is an apparent violation of the law (logging is not exempted as a categorical exclusion), yet the agency is not being forced into compliance. Even those federal agencies doing an adequate job of field inspection for Section 106 purposes may not be complying with the legally required, full-scale inventory of their lands (Section 110 of the NHPA, the Archaeological Resource Protection Act). In the absence of federal or state enforcement, it is likely that litigation would be the only way to press these issues.

Some of the most contentious arguments have arisen over a fundamental question: can someone be disbarred from doing archaeology and, if so, how? An obvious solution is licensure, with specified conditions for how licenses to practice archaeology can be obtained and renewed or revoked if review by a designated body (such as the SHPO) documents malfeasance or incompetent work. There is ample precedent for such a requirement, in geology, engineering, medicine, and other fields. Attempts to license archaeologists have fallen flat, however, primarily because of reluctance on the part of state lawmakers to add bureaucratic burdens to development and partly, one suspects, because archaeology is still perceived as an anachronistic undertaking rather than a legitimate discipline comparable to other fields. Also, many archaeologists apparently prefer the looseness of the status quo and vocally resist attempts to impose a licensure system.

It was because of such problems that the Register of Professional Archaeologists (RPA) was established in 1998. Formerly the Society of Professional Archaeologists, the Register is "[...] a listing of archaeologists who have agreed to abide by an explicit code of conduct and standards of research performance, who hold a graduate degree in archaeology, anthropology, art history, classics, history, or other germane discipline and who have substantial practical experience". "A hallmark of the Register [...] is a formal grievance procedure that allows for the investigation of complaints about the professional conduct of an RPA. If an allegation of a violation of the code of standards is supported during an investigation, sanctions, including termination of registrations, can be given. Fair investigation and efforts at resolution through mediation always precede any formal proceedings" (http://www.rpanet.org/about.htm).

The register is sponsored by the major archaeological organizations in the US (the Society for Historical Archaeology, the Society for American Archaeology, the Archaeological Institute of America): its code (http://www.rpanet.org/conduct.htm) contains general rules for conduct that all professional archaeologists should be in agreement with. An obvious solution to a number of problems, therefore, would be for states to adopt RPA membership as a requirement for doing CRM. Such an action would absolve SHPO's of the responsibility for enforcement in many of the areas discussed above. Yet this has not happened, partly because of the vocal resistance mentioned above and partly because states are wary of legal challenges to such a requirement. In 1999, Mississippi became the first state to adopt a formal RPA requirement for doing CRM, an achievement made possible by very hard work on the part of certain SHPO staff and one endorsed by the state's professional archaeological association. This "quiet revolution [...] place[d] archaeology in the same class as Certified Public Accountants and Registered Professional Engineers" (McClung 2000, 1–2).

The requirement was soon rescinded, however, when an individual doing CRM in the state complained (even though that individual was qualified to become an RPA). Efforts to accommodate the individual by, for example, inserting a 'grandfather clause' in the requirement, were of no avail: the state refused to consider any compromise offered by the president of the Register or other parties. Instead, a letter was sent out by the SHPO stating that the requirement "would exceed those of the Secretary of Interior's Standards and Guidelines and therefore exceed the standards that the Federal Government requires" (Hilliard 2001). Why this should be a problem for states, which may enact legislation for resource management that exceeds federal requirements, was not explained. The 'quiet revolution' was thus overturned by a single, not-so-quiet CRM archaeologist, despite numerous entreaties by other professionals in the state.

DISCUSSION

In addition to the problems discussed in this paper, there are other QA concerns in American archaeology, including the perennial lack of dissemination of results from CRM, the continuing looting of sites (*cf.* Brodie and Renfrew 2005; Mathers, Schelberg and Kneebone 2005), the relatively low proportion of National Register-listed properties that are archaeological sites (Little 2005; Mathers, Schelberg and Kneebone 2005, 161), and so on. Space restrictions preclude discussion of these, but it is hoped that this volume will encourage a much-needed debate about QA in archaeology at a global scale. Some suggestions can be made for improving the situation as it currently exists in the US.

Archaeologists must pay more attention to contexts that have come to be automatically disregarded in CRM (figure 9.4). This refers primarily to surface/plowzone contexts. The assumption that nothing of importance can be learned from artifacts retrieved from such contexts is not justified: recent field studies have demonstrated the utility of controlled surface collections on plowed sites for delineating individual occupations, for example (Rafferty 2001). Those occupations can then be treated as units of analysis in lieu of the more traditional components. If controlled surface investigations, coupled with limited subsurface testing (*e.g.* coring), reveal that only one occupation is present, then it may be assumed that a representative sample from that occupation has been obtained and decisions about stripping will be that much more informed.

A clear problem in US CRM is the variability in adherence to laws, regulations, and guidelines. Laws and regulations should be enforced at the state and federal levels, and it is not acceptable to disregard 'guidelines' as suggestions that need not be followed: if guidelines can be ignored, they are not needed. If they are needed, they should not be ignored. At a minimum, all federal and state agencies should insure that all field and lab work is conducted or directly supervised solely by individuals who meet the Secretary of Interior's standards for professional qualifications. The OPM standards should be revised accordingly.

Figure 9.4 Gravel debitage collected from the surface of a small site in northern Mississippi. No artifacts diagnostic of any particular cultural period are present. Such 'lithic scatters' tend to be automatically disregarded as unimportant, when in fact site age, function, duration, and other attributes are unknown without further work.

In the US, much decision-making power is delegated to states (*e.g.* US Department of the Interior 1980) and is codified in the Statewide Historic Preservation Plans created under a provision of the NHPA (Noble 1987; Wendorf 1980). Different states have different permitting procedures for work conducted on state land (*e.g.* Sprinkle 1998). States may exceed federal requirements or may use them to stymie efforts to change the system, as in the Mississippi example described earlier. The tension between economic development and resource protection is most pronounced at the state level. A bill recently introduced in Utah, for example, would do away with the office of State Archaeologist and lower the standards for project review. Supporters of the bill contend it would expedite energy development in the state. No doubt. It doubtless would also expedite the destruction of sites, including 'minor' sites characterized by the bill's author, Representative Bradley T. Johnson, as "chippings or whatever it is" (http://www.ksl.com/index.php). In the current political climate of the US there is an unbridled antagonism against science that is seen as retarding development. Until archaeology is better appreciated as a science, it will be particularly vulnerable to such attacks. If for no other reason, promoting CRM as a purely technical practice is dangerous for this reason.

Is CRM research? We would argue that it is because, while it involves the employment of a set range of practical skills to retrieve materials remains, decisions about what remains to recover, how they will be recovered, and what they will be used for all, are research-based questions. Also, the only practical way to address the fact that current research questions cannot account for future research needs is to preserve/ recover/curate a representative sample of everything that's out there (Dixon 1977; Dunnell 1984; Glassow 1977; Hickman 1977; Lipe 1974; Mathers, Schelberg and Kneebone 2005; Peacock 1996; Plog 1981; Smith 2005), an approach that also can be adopted for non-scientific concerns (Baugher 2005; Funari 2005, 127; Lilley and Williams 2005; Little 2005, 118; Mathers, Schelberg and Kneebone 2005; Peacock 1996; Peacock and Patrick 1997; Smith 2005; Swidler and Yeatts 2005). Learning how to recognize and to recover that variability is as important a realm of research as anything that archaeologists do (*cf.* Stahl 1999; Tainter and Bagley 2005). It demands imagination and reflexivity. It cannot be done by continuing to employ traditional artifact typologies and space/time constructs derived from culture history. It demands a renewed attention to theory, the questions that flow from theory, and the methods that flow from the questions (*cf.* Altschul 2005). CRM – or CRM as it should be practiced – is not simply a technical skill: it is brain-work.

As Knudson (1986), King (2004), and others have noted, CRM involves much more than archaeology. It requires knowledge of environmental factors, natural resources, architecture, and traditional lifeways: it demands political skills, management skills, writing skills, and more. Increasingly, it demands extensive knowledge of Geographical Information Systems, Global Positioning Systems, geophysical instrumentation, and other technology. All of this must be coupled with the ability to think critically, to identify and solve problems, to make decisions that are based in theory rather than rote practice. Graduate programs must be flexible in such regards, and allow students to obtain credit in classes that will help broaden their perspective outside of the typical archaeological or anthropological realms. But the archaeology cannot be shorted in this process. While most schools teach a field school in excavation, precious few provide formal training in archaeological survey. The defense that "anyone can dig holes in the ground" (a comment made by an academic archaeologist in the southeastern US who also engages in CRM) is ludicrous, given the complexity of the record and the contexts in which it is contained. Much, if not most, of the work that CRM archaeologists do is done at the phase I level, and it is at that level that most of the decisions take place about which sites are not significant and can be destroyed. Surely some formal training in this process should be required? Teaching a survey field school is relatively easy and inexpensive; developing a training curriculum for geophysics is more expensive, but will become increasingly necessary as the full potential of such technology is realized. All of this should be linked to theory, so that technology is not seen as a replacement for thinking about how and why we do things the way we do, and how and why they might be done better.

It would be hubris to suggest that any one theoretical approach should dominate where archaeology in general or CRM in particular is concerned, but it is worth pointing out that evolutionary theory is predicated upon the recognition and explanation of variability. Evolutionary archaeology thus provides an alternative to more traditional approaches that have become mired in typological thinking, which results in the rote categorization of sites and artifacts. It is distinct from the progressive cultural evolution that still pervades much of American archaeology. Stahl (1999) and Tainter and Bagley (2005) have recently provided a critique of how progressivist models limit the perception of variability in the archaeological record, a critique with which we are in agreement (*cf.* Peacock and Hogue 2005). Culture-historians, processual archaeologists, and others would do well to consider the theoretical challenges raised by evolutionary archaeology rather than simply dismissing them as iconoclastic (*e.g.* Williams 2003). Whatever emerges from such a debate would likely be more robust and defensible than current practice, and the results would benefit CRM from both a practical and a scientific standpoint.

ACKNOWLEDGEMENTS

We would like to thank the many outstanding professionals working for state or federal agencies who provided information used in this chapter. We also would like to thank Willem Willems for inviting us to contribute to this volume. Support for this research was provided by Dr. Joe Seger, director of the Cobb Institute of Archaeology, Mississippi State University.

References

Altschul, J. H. (2005) Significance in American Cultural Resource Management. In C. Mathers, T. Darvill and B. J. Little (eds) *Heritage of Value, Archaeology of Renown: Reshaping Archaeological Assessment and Significance*, 192–210. Gainesville.

Baugher, S. (2005) Sacredness, Sensitivity and Significance: The Controversy over Native American Sacred Sites. In C. Mathers, T. Darvill and B. J. Little (eds) *Heritage of Value, Archaeology of Renown: Reshaping Archaeological Assessment and Significance*, 248–275. Gainesville.

Binford, L. R. (1964) A Consideration of Archaeological Research Design. *American Antiquity* 45, 551–553.

Briuer, F. L. (1996) Toward a Holistic Approach to Significance Evaluation: Introductory Comments on the Workshop Papers. In F. L. Briuer (ed.) *Cultural Resource Significance Evaluation: Proceedings of a US Army Corps of Engineers Workshop, 3–4 October 1994, Vicksburg, Mississippi*, 1–11. (US Army Corps of Engineers, Water Resources Support Center, Institute for Water Resources, IWR Report 96–EL-3). Alexandria.

Briuer, F. L. and C. Mathers (1996) *Trends and Patters in Cultural Resource Significance: An Historical Perspective and Annotated Bibliography*. (US Army Corps of Engineers, Water Resources Support Center, Institute for Water Resources, IWR Report 96–EL-1). Alexandria.

Brodie, N. and C. Renfrew (2005) Looting and the World's Archaeological Heritage: The Inadequate Response. *Annual Review of Anthropology* 34, 343–361.

Butler, W. B. (1987) Significance and Other Frustrations in the CRM Process. *American Antiquity* 52, 820–829.

Chapman, S., R. Walling, L. Seago and P. D. Jackson (1999) *Cultural Resource Survey, Rehabilitation and Repairs, Sterlington to Monroe, and Testing of 16OU97, Ouachita River Levees, Louisiana*. (Report submitted to the US Army Corps of Engineers, Vicksburg District, by Panamerican Consultants, Inc.). Memphis.

Connaway, J. M. and S. O. McGahey (1971) *Archaeological Excavation at the Boyd Site, Tunica County, Mississippi*. (Mississippi Department of Archives and History, Technical Report Number 1). Jackson.

Dancey, W. S. (1998) The Value of Surface Archaeological Data in Exploring the Dynamics of Community Evolution in the Middle Ohio Valley. In A. P. Sullivan III (ed.) *Surface Archaeology*, 3–19. Albuquerque.

Darvill, T. (2005) "Sorted for Ease and Whiz?" Approaching Value and Importance in Archaeological Resource Management. In C. Mathers, T. Darvill and B. J. Little (eds) *Heritage of Value, Archaeology of Renown: Reshaping Archaeological Assessment and Significance*, 21–42. Gainesville.

Dixon, K. A. (1977) Applications of Archaeological Resources: Broadening the Basis of Significance. In M. B. Schiffer and G. J. Gumerman (eds) *Conservation Archaeology: A Guide for Cultural Resource Management Studies*, 277–290. New York.

Dunnell, R. C. (1982) Science, Social Science, and Common Sense: The Agonizing Dilemma of Modern Archaeology. *Journal of Anthropological Research* 38(1), 1–25.

Dunnell, R. C. (1984) The Ethics of Archaeological Significance Decisions. In E. L. Green (ed.) *Ethics and Values in Archaeology*, 62–74. New York.

Fisher, C. (1980) Significance Evaluations of Low Density Surface Sites: Another View. *Journal of Field Archaeology* 7, 498–499.

Fox, G. L. (1998) An Examination of Mississippian-Period Phases in Southeastern Missouri. In M. J. O'Brien and R. C. Dunnell (eds) *Changing Perspectives on the Archaeology of the Central Mississippi Valley*, 31–58. Tuscaloosa.

Funari, P. P. A. (2005) Reassessing Archaeological Significance: Heritage of Value and Archaeology of Renown in Brazil. In C. Mathers, T. Darvill and B. J. Little (eds) *Heritage of Value, Archaeology of Renown: Reshaping Archaeological Assessment and Significance*, 125–136. Gainesville.

Glassow, M. A. (1977) Comment on Schiffer and House. *Current Anthropology* 18, 56.

Green, Th. J. (1983) Strategies for the Preservation of Archaeological Sites in Idaho. *Idaho Archaeologist* 6(3), 1–3.

Grün, R., C. B. Stringer and H. P. Schwarcz (1991) ESR Dating of Teeth from Garrod's Tabun Cave Collection. *Journal of Human Evolution* 20, 231–248.

Hardesty, D. L. and B. J. Little (2000) *Assessing Site Significance: A Guide for Archaeologists and Historians*. Walnut Creek, California.

Hickman, P. Parker (1977) Problems of Significance: Two Case Studies of Historical Sites. In M. B. Schiffer and G. J. Gumerman (eds) *Conservation Archaeology: A Guide for Cultural Resource Management Studies*, 269–275. New York.

Hilliard, E. R. (2001) Letter to Archaeological Consultants. (On file, Mississippi Department of Archives and History). Jackson.

Hutt, S., E. W. Jones and M. E. McAllister (1992) *Archeological Resource Protection*. Washington D.C.

King, Th. F. (2004) *Cultural Resource Laws and Practice*. (Second edition). Walnut Creek.

King, Th. F. (2005) *Doing Archaeology: A Cultural Resource Management Perspective*. Walnut Creek.

Knudson, R. (1986) Contemporary Cultural Resource Management. In D. J. Meltzer, D. D. Fowler and J. A. Sabloff (eds) *American Archaeology Past and Future*, 395–413. Washington D.C.

Kuttruff, C., M. Hutchins, D. B. Kelley and L. A. Wilkie (1995) *Archaeological Test Excavations at Eight Sites in the Upper Steele Bayou Basin, Washington County, Mississippi*. (Report submitted to U.S. Army Corps of Engineers, Vicksburg District by Coastal Environments, Inc.). Baton Rouge.

Lilley, I. and M. Williams (2005) Archaeological and Indigenous Significance: A View from Australia. In C. Mathers, T. Darvill and B. J. Little (eds) *Heritage of Value, Archaeology of Renown: Reshaping Archaeological Assessment and Significance*, 227–247. Gainesville.

Lipe, W. D. (1974) A Conservation Model for American Archaeology. *The Kiva* 39, 213–245.

Lipe, W. D. (1978) Contracts, Bureaucrats and Research: Some Emerging Problems of Conservation Archaeology in the United States. In R. C. Dunnell and E. S. Hall Jr. (eds) *Archaeological Essays in Honor of Irving B. Rouse*, 121–147. The Hague.

Lipo, C. P., M. E. Madsen, R. C. Dunnell and T. Hunt (1997) Population Structure, Cultural Transmission and Frequency Seriation. *Journal of Anthropological Archaeology* 6, 301–333.

Little, B. J. (2005) The U.S. National Register of Historic Places and the Shaping of Archaeological Significance. In C. Mathers, T. Darvill and B. J. Little (eds) *Heritage of Value, Archaeology of Renown: Reshaping Archaeological Assessment and Significance*, 114–124. Gainesville.

Lyman, R. L., M. J. O'Brien and R. C. Dunnell (eds) (1997) *Americanist Culture History: Fundamentals of Time, Space and Form*. New York.

Lynott, M. J. (1980) The Dynamics of Significance: An Example from Central Texas. *American Antiquity* 45, 117–120.

Lyon, E. A. (1996) *A New Deal for Southeastern Archaeology*. Tuscaloosa.

Mathers, C., T. Darvill and B. J. Little (2005) Introduction: Archaeological Value in a World Context. In C. Mathers, T. Darvill and B. J. Little (eds) *Heritage of Value, Archaeology of Renown: Reshaping Archaeological Assessment and Significance*, 1–18. Gainesville.

Mathers, C., J. Schelberg and R. Kneebone (2005) "Drawing Distinctions": Toward a Scalar Model of Value and Significance. In C. Mathers, T. Darvill and B. J. Little (eds) *Heritage of Value, Archaeology of Renown: Reshaping Archaeological Assessment and Significance*, 159–191. Gainesville.

McClung, T. (2000) The Plow Zone. *Mississippi Archaeological Association Newsletter* 35(1), 1–2. Jackson

McGimsey, Ch. R. III and H. A. Davis (eds) (1977) *The Management of Archaeological Resources: The Airlie House Report*. Washington D.C.

McManamon, F. P. (1977) Comment on Schiffer and House. *Current Anthropology* 18, 58.

McManamon, F. P. (1990) A Regional Perspective on Assessing the Significance of Historic Period Sites. *Historical Archaeology* 24(2), 14–22.

McMillan, B., M. Grady and W. Lipe (1977) Cultural Resource Management. In Ch. R. McGimsey III and H. A. Davis (eds) *The Management of Archaeological Resources: The Airlie House Report*, 25–63. Washington D.C.

Meighan, C. W. (1986) *Archaeology for Money*. Calabasas, California.

Moeller, R. W. (1992) *Analyzing and Interpreting Late Woodland Features*. (Archaeological Services, Occasional Publications in Northeastern Anthropology No. 12). Bethlehem.

Moratto, M. J. and R. E. Kelly (1978) Optimizing Strategies for Evaluating Archaeological Significance. In M. B. Schiffer (ed.) *Advances in Archaeological Method and Theory*, Vol. 1, 1–30. New York.

Neumann, Th. W. and R. M. Sanford (2001) *Cultural Resources Archaeology: An Introduction*. Walnut Creek, California.

Noble, V. E. (1987) A Problem of Preservation: Assessing Significance of Historic Cultural Resources in Illinois. In T. E. Emerson and C. L. Rohrbaugh (eds) *Nineteenth Century Historic Archaeology in Illinois*, 33–43. Springfield.

O'Brien, M. J. and R. L. Lyman (2003) Style, Function, Transmission: An Introdution. In M. J. O'Brien and R. L. Lyman (eds) *Style, Function, Transmission: Evolutionary Archaeological Perspectives*, 1–32. Salt Lake City.

Peacock, E. (1994) *Cultural Resources Inventory, Timber Thinning Areas, Fiscal Year 1994, Bayou Bodcau Reservoir, Bossier and Webster Parishes, Louisiana.* (Report submitted to the U.S. Army Corps of Engineers, Vicksburg District, by Panamerican Consultants, Inc.). Tuscaloosa.

Peacock, E. (1996) Some Comments on Significance and Federal Archaeology. In F. L. Briuer (ed.) *Cultural Resource Significance Evaluation: Proceedings of a U.S. Army Corps of Engineers Workshop, 3–4 October 1994, Vicksburg, Mississippi*, 42–50. (U.S. Army Corps of Engineers, Water Resources Support Center, Institute for Water Resources, IWR Report 96–EL-3). Alexandria.

Peacock, E. and S. H. Hogue (2005) A New Series of Absolute Dates from Lyon's Bluff (22OK520), East-Central Mississippi. *Southeastern Archaeology* 24, 46–58.

Peacock, E. and A. J. Patrick (1997) Site Survey and Land-Records Research: A Comparison of Two Methods for Locating and Characterizing Historic Period Sites on the Tombigbee National Forest, Mississippi. *Mississippi Archaeology* 32,1–26.

Peacock, E., J. Rafferty and S. H. Hogue (2005) Land Snails, Artifacts and Faunal Remains: Understanding Site Formation Processes at Prehistoric/Protohistoric Sites in the Southeastern United States. In D. E. Bar-Yosef (ed.) *Archaeomalacology: Molluscs in Former Environments of Human Behaviour*, 6–17. Oxford.

Pickens, S. S. (1998) The Silent Criteria: Misuse and Abuse of the National Register. In M. A. Tomlan (ed.) *Preservation of What, for Whom? A Critical Look at Historical Significance*, 193–202. Ithaca.

Plog, F. (1981) *Cultural Resources Overview, Little Colorado Area, Arizona.* Washington D.C.

Raab, L. M. and T. C. Klinger (1977) A Critical Appraisal of Significance in Contract Archaeology. *American Antiquity* 42, 629–634.

Raab, L. M. and T. C. Klinger (1979) A Reply to Sharrock and Grayson on Archaeological Significance. *American Antiquity* 44, 328–329.

Rafferty, J. (1986) A Critique of the Type-Variety System as Used in Ceramic Analysis. *Mississippi Archaeology* 21(2), 40–50.

Rafferty, J. (2001) Determining Duration at Prehistoric Sites: Short-Term Sedentary Settlement at Josey Farm, NE Mississippi. *Journal of Field Archaeology* 28, 347–366.

Raffino, R. A. (1977) Comment on Schiffer and House. *Current Anthropology* 18, 59–60.

Reed, A. D. (1987) A Technique for Ranking Prehistoric Sites in Terms of Scientific Significance. *American Archaeology* 6(2), 127–130.

Schaafsma, C. F. (1989) Significant Until Proven Otherwise: Problems Versus Representative Samples. In H. Cleere (ed.) *Archaeological Heritage Management in the Modern World*, 38–51. London.

Schiffer, M. B. and G. J. Gumerman (eds) (1977) *Conservation Archaeology: A Guide for Cultural Resource Management Studies.* New York.

Schiffer, M. B. and J. H. House (Assemblers) (1975) *The Cache River Archeological Project: An Experiment in Contract Archeology.* (Arkansas Archeological Survey Research Series 8). Fayetteville.

Schiffer, M. B. and J. H. House (1977) Cultural Resource Management and Archaeological Research: The Cache Project. *Current Anthropology* 18, 43–68.

Scott, D. D. (1990) Site Significance and Historical Archaeology – A Scenario and Commentary. *Historical Archaeology* 24(2), 52–54.

Scovill, D. H., G. J. Gordon and K. M. Anderson (1972) *Guidelines for the Preparation of Statements of Environmental Impact on Archeological Resources.* Tucson.

Sharrock, F. W. and D. K. Grayson (1979) "Significance" in Contract Archaeology. *American Antiquity* 44, 327–328.

Smith, L. (2005) Archaeological Significance and the Governance of Identity in Cultural Heritage Management. In C. Mathers, T. Darvill and B. J. Little (eds) *Heritage of Value, Archaeology of Renown: Reshaping Archaeological Assessment and Significance*, 77–88. Gainesville.

Sprinkle, J. H. (Jr) (1998) Do Archaeologists Dig, Destroy, and Discriminate? The Historical Significance and Value of Archaeological Sites. In M. A. Tomlan (ed.) *Preservation of What, for Whom? A Critical Look at Historical Significance*, 169–178. Ithaca.

Stahl, A. B. (1999) Perceiving Variability in Time and Space: The Evolutionary Mapping of African Societies. In S. K. McIntosh (ed.) *Beyond Chiefdoms: Pathways to Complexity in Africa*, 39–55. Cambridge.

Stuart, D. E. and R. P. Gauthier (1981) *Prehistoric New Mexico: Background for Survey*. Santa Fe.

Sullivan, A. P., III (ed.) (1998) *Surface Archaeology*. Albuquerque.

Swidler, N. and M. Yeatts (2005) Traditional Cultural Properties and the National Preservation Program in the United States. In C. Mathers, T. Darvill and B. J. Little (eds) *Heritage of Value, Archaeology of Renown: Reshaping Archaeological Assessment and Significance*, 276–286. Gainesville.

Tainter, J. A. (1979) The Mountainair Lithic Scatters: Settlement Patterns and Significance Evaluation of Low Density Surface Sites. *Journal of Field Archaeology* 6, 463–469.

Tainter, J. A. (1987) The Politics of Regional Research in Conservation Archaeology. *American Archaeology* 6(3), 217–227.

Tainter, J. A. and B. Bagley (2005) Shaping and Suppressing the Archaeological Record: Significance in American Cultural Resource Management. In C. Mathers, T. Darvill and B. J. Little (eds) *Heritage of Value, Archaeology of Renown: Reshaping Archaeological Assessment and Significance*, 58–73. Gainesville.

Tainter, J. A. and G. J. Lucas (1983) Epistemology of the Significance Concept. *American Antiquity* 48, 707–719.

Thacker, P. T., B. B. Ellwood and C. M. C. Pereira (2001) Detecting Palaeolithic Activity Areas through Electrical Resistivity Survey: An Assessment from Vale de Óbidos, Portugal. *Journal of Archaeological Science* 29, 563–570.

Tomlan, M. A. (ed.) (1998) *Preservation of What, for Whom? A Critical Look at Historical Significance*. Ithaca.

U.S. Department of Agriculture, Forest Service, the Mississippi Department of Archives and History, and the Advisory Council on Historic Preservation (1996) *Memorandum of Understanding Concerning the Management of Heritage Resources in the National Forests in Mississippi.* (On file, US Forest Service Office). Jackson.

U.S. Department of Agriculture, Natural Resources Conservation Service, the Advisory Council on Historic Preservation, and the National Conference of State Historic Preservation Officers (2002) *Programmatic Agreement Relative to Conservation Assistance*. (Natural Resources Conservation Service, document NRCA A-3A75–2–64). Washington D.C.

U.S. Department of the Interior (1980) *Resource Protection Planning Process*. Heritage Conservation and Recreation Service Publication No. 50 (Preservation Planning Series). (U.S. Department of the Interior, Heritage Conservation and Recreation Service, Division of State Plans and Grants). Washington D.C.

U.S. Office of Personnel Management (1983) *Position Classification Standard for Archeology Series*, GS-0193. (U.S. Office of Personnel Management, TS-70). Washington D.C.

Weaver, G. G., M. R. Childress, C. A. Buchner and M. E. Starr (1996) *Archaeological Investigations at Three Sites Near Arlington, State Route 385 (Paul Barrett Parkway), Shelby County, Tennessee: Phase II Testing at 40SY525 and 40SY526 and Phase III Data Recovery at 40SY527*. (Report submitted to the

Tennessee Department of Transportation, Nashville, by Garrow and Associates). Memphis.
Wendorf, F. (1980) The Fort Burgwin Report. *Journal of Field Archaeology* 7, 248–253.
Wettstaed, J. (2002) Difficulties with Archaeological Units in the Missouri Ozarks. *The Missouri Archaeologist* 63, 83–104.
Willey, G. R. and Ph. Phillips (2001) *Method and Theory in American Archaeology*. (Originally published in 1958 by The University of Chicago Press). Tuscaloosa.
Williams, S. (2003) Introduction to the 2003 Edition. In Ph. Phillips, J. A. Ford and J. B. Griffin (eds) *Archaeological Survey in the Lower Mississippi Alluvial Valley, 1940–1947*, xi–xxxii. (Original edition published in 1951 by the Peabody Museum of American Archaeology and Ethnology, Harvard University). Tuscaloosa.
Wilson, J. S. (1990) We've Got Thousands of These? What Makes an Historic Farmstead Significant? *Historical Archaeology* 24(2), 23–33.
Wood, W. R. (2002) The Realities of Ethnogenesis. *The Missouri Archaeologist* 63, 71–82.

CHAPTER 10

Scientific quality control and the general organisation of French archaeology

Jean Paul Demoule

INTRODUCTION

Debate over the quality control of archaeological excavation has only been seriously raised during the last few years. It stems from the emergence of private archaeological firms, which have expanded to such an extent that in some countries, for example the United States of America, it seems that inadequate control has led to important scientific, even financial, waste.

From this point of view, quality control is discussed in a fundamentally different way according to whether there exists, in a given country, a commercial private archaeology. For the last twenty or so years, in many countries, particularly within the European Union, a certain number of economic activities have been ceded by the State to the 'market economy'. As a result, there is sometimes a tendency to consider that this evolution should from now on concern the whole of the activities of a society and should constitute the only way of envisaging these activities. This state of affairs explains why there are, sometimes, within the community of European archaeologists, some difficulties of understanding.

A LITTLE HISTORY

For us archaeologists, and thus also historians and anthropologists, it is thus worthwhile to recall some historical and cultural facts. In the western world there are two contrasting concepts of society. In one of them, the tradition of Roman Law, given new life by the French 'Civil Code', the State, in its role as the expression of the community of citizens, organises and regulates social life. In the other, based on the tradition of Anglo-Saxon Common Law, society regulates itself either, in Adam Smith's optimistic version, under the effect of a 'hidden hand', or, in the pessimistic versions of Neo-Darwinism, of socio-biology, and of economic liberalism in general, by means of the 'struggle for life'. As with everything in this world, each of these conceptions has its advantages and its drawbacks. At the level of generality, too much state intervention leads to a state of immobilism, too much liberalism leads to disorder and increasing inequalities. But, as historians and anthropologists, archaeologists should not forget, in both cases it is primarily a question of cultural constructs.

In western countries, from the moment that archaeology became a fully-fledged science and insofar as its results could interest ideology and national culture, the archaeologist was placed under the control of the nation. More concretely, from the middle of the 19th century national archaeological services were set up as were national museums – supplemented by regional archaeological services and regional museums. Archaeological excavations became subject to authorisations. Historical monuments and archaeological sites were placed under the protection of the State. This conception became imperative in almost all European countries, most of which still regard it as self-evidently correct. The differences are only matters of detail and, above all, from the second half of the 20th century, that of the financing of rescue archaeology excavations. Should the costs be borne by the State, given their duty to protect the heritage, or should the developer, responsible for the destruction of the archaeological site, pay, assuming that the destruction was unavoidable?

From the 1980s, things began to change on the Atlantic fringes of Europe, with the increasing domination, first of all economic, then political and finally cultural and ideological, of the United States of America. This increasing ideological domination, that of ultra-liberalism, was more or less incarnated in America's president Ronald Reagan, and the British prime minister Margaret Thatcher. In the United States, archaeology, considered as the search for and exaltation of ancestors, has never been a strong ideological issue. After all, non-native Americans knew perfectly well that they had come from Europe (or from Africa). There was thus no need, for a large part of the territory, for an authorisation to excavate and there was no general system of protection for material culture of the past. That is why, as soon as rescue excavations became obligatory, at least in Federal public works projects, as early as the 1970s, forms of private archaeology effortlessly established themselves in a pattern of competing commercial companies. In the early stages, as is well known, this wild-cat competition brought about a number of losses, not only of wasted money, but also of archaeological information and scientific evidence, before a minimal schema of professional regulation was gradually introduced. There still exists, nonetheless, a fairly wide gulf between cultural resource management (CRM) and traditional academic archaeology.

From America, during the 1980s, this model was progressively introduced into Britain, a country whose archaeological practice had, until then, been considered as a model (and certainly by many French archaeologists). Step by step, a system of private commercial archaeology was set up. It is not my intention here to evaluate its efficiency from a scientific point of view. Nonetheless, it is a phenomenon whose sheer scale makes it unique to Britain. Ostensibly, commercial and private companies exist in other western countries, but in reality they are seldom truly competing with one another. In the German *Länder* or the Swiss *cantons* for example, it is the regional archaeological services that choose their firm. This fact became very obvious during the annual congress of the European Association of Archaeologists (EAA), during September 2000, at Lisbon, which I organised with Willem Willems, the then president of the Association, concerning archaeological legislation in Europe. Most of the time, differences of conception and organisation opposed Great Britain and the rest of Europe! This difference appeared again during the meeting organised at Vilnius in Lithuania in December 2004 in the context of the EPAC network (European Preventive Archaeology Corpus).

GENERAL ORGANISATION OF ARCHAEOLOGY IN FRANCE

Preventive archaeology in France is organised by the Law of 17th January 2001, modified in 2003 and 2004, which constitutes the application to French law of the European Convention of the Protection of the Archaeological Heritage of Valletta (Malta) in 1992, ratified by France in 1994. This law is based on two principles: the developer pays for preventive archaeology ('polluter pays'), and most of this activity is entrusted to an institute of public research, the Institut National de Recherches Archéologiques Preventives (INRAP), under the double supervision of the Ministry of Culture and of the Ministry of Research. INRAP's budget is approximately € 115 million, *i.e.* 0.1% of the total budget of construction and public works in France.

There are about 3000 archaeologists in France, just over half of whom work within INRAP; the others are shared fairly equally between the universities (archaeology is studied in about fifteen universities), the Centre National de la Recherche Scientifique (CNRS), the Ministry of Culture (with its sub-department of Central Archaeology and the regional archaeological services on the one hand, as well as the curators of archaeological museums), and lastly the archaeologists of towns and *départements*. There are about twenty 'private' archaeologists, partly in associative structures (non-profit-making organisations). The population of France is 63 million, so there is about one archaeologist per 20,000 inhabitants. This places France below the European average, and beneath countries such as Greece, Switzerland and the United Kingdom.

The Ministry of Culture, through its Regional Archaeological Services (SRA) is the one who authorises archaeological excavations. In the case of preventive archaeology, the SRA prescribes the undertaking of 'diagnostics', to detect, identify and evaluate archaeological remains in an area due for development. As the case arises, the SRA prescribes full-fledged excavations. The Ministry of Culture is advised by a scientific council, the Conseil National de la Recherche Archéologique (CNRA) presided by the minister. At a regional level, councils of experts, the Commissions Interrégionales de la Recherche Archéologique (CIRA) give advice to the regional archaeological services.

INRAP, as a research institute answerable both to the Ministry of Culture and the Ministry of Research, also comprises a Scientific Council, two thirds of which are experts elected by the archaeologists of various institutions. Most of its members are archaeologists from outside INRAP. Apart from administrative departments, INRAP also has a scientific department which defines the scientific policy of the establishment. On the regional level, INRAP includes a certain number

Figure 10.1 Archaeological trial trenches before a road project in France (Photo INRAP).

of interregional departments, whose directors are helped by scientific assistants, responsible for the control at a local level of the scientific quality of work in the field, as well as the publication of studies, but also the collaboration with other scientific institutions. More generally, INRAP has passed a number of conventions of cooperation with the CNRS, the universities, the archaeological services of the towns or the *départements*, and even some foreign institutions.

The Archaeological Map of the Ministry of Culture indicates approximately 400,000 sites – whereas forecasts from the best-known areas estimate potential sites at several million (doubtless between 5 and 10 million). On the great motorway and railway axes, where trial excavations are systematic (figure 10.1), an important site is found at every kilometre. Each year about 70,000 hectares (700 km^2) are subjected to development projects (constructions, motorways, TGV, quarries, industrial zones, underground car parks, etc.), and this does not include the 'invisible' but very worrying destructions caused by agricultural and forest works. Of these 70,000 hectares, about 15% are subjected to 'diagnostics' prescribed by the regional services of the Ministry of Culture, representing about 2000 operations a year, or 90,000 working days.

TRIAL EXCAVATIONS AND THEIR CONTROL

According to law, diagnostic evaluations are a public monopoly, shared between INRAP (for about 95%) and the archaeological services of towns and *départements* that desire it. This public monopoly is destined, according to the words of the Minister of Culture, to guarantee the objectivity of the evaluations – in other words to avoid the situation of private enterprises, under pressure from the developers, specialising in finding nothing! Evaluations are financed by a tax paid by all developers, whether or not there is an archaeological site on their land. This tax should theoretically bring in between € 60 and € 80 million per year, but it is not, as yet, completely finalised in its application. A third of this tax is intended for a fund to help small developers to pay for the cost of the full-fledged excavations, when required.

In France, the great majority of diagnostic evaluations are carried out by mechanically excavating trenches to an area of between 5% and 10% of the total surface, which constitutes a minimum statistical threshold. Aerial photographs and diverse other 'non-intrusive' techniques are used, but only in specific cases. Prehistoric sites in particular are likely to be uncovered only through such systematic trenching. It is striking that for several years a certain number of Lower and Middle Palaeolithic sites have been discovered in the North-West of France through this technique, while they are unknown in the South-East of England, an area perfectly comparable from a geological or archaeological point of view but where this technique is not used.

According to the organisation described above, diagnostic evaluations are the object of a double control of scientific quality. The internal control is carried out by the regional scientific assistant of INRAP, in liaison with the national scientific department and the national scientific council. The external control is carried out by the regional archaeological service of the Ministry of Culture, aided by the Commission Interrégionale de la Recherche Archéologique (CIRA) and, if need be, in the case of important sites where serious problems have been encountered, by the Conseil National de la Recherche Archéologique (CNRA). Only when the results of the evaluations are known, do the services of the Ministry of Culture decide if there should be further excavations or not. Between 20% and 25% of the diagnostic evaluations are followed by full-fledged excavations (figure 10.2).

ARCHAEOLOGICAL EXCAVATIONS AND THEIR CONTROL

According to the terms of the initial law of 2001, excavations are also a public monopoly and entrusted to INRAP with the obligation for the latter to cooperate with other scientific institutions as necessary. This stipulation was challenged at the Commission of the European Union, Brussels, by certain private archaeologists and some developers. By a decision dated April 2nd 2003, the Commission rejected

Figure 10.2 The Neolithic site of Bucy-le-Long (France) after removing the top soil (Photo INRAP).

this complaint. This decision is of great importance: it signifies that each member country of the European Union can, if it wishes, organise its preventive archaeology as a public monopoly and that, in this domain at least, the 'free market economy' is neither a necessity nor an inevitability (for a more complete legal analysis in French, *cf.* Demoule 2004; for a previous English introduction, *cf.* Demoule 2002).

Nevertheless, the new parliamentary majority in 2003 amended the initial 2001 law by introducing the possibility for the developer himself to enter into commercial competition for the excavations. This modification reflected the political sensibility, economically liberal, of this new majority. It also expressed the hope of lowering the excavation costs by introducing commercial competition, a hope that has not been realised.

This introduction of commercial competition was nonetheless accompanied by various precautions. The private enterprises are subjected to a scientific approval, renewable every five years, after examination of their dossier by the Conseil National de la Recherche Archéologique. They cannot be economically dependent on the developers. The excavation plans of the developer's subcontractor have to be submitted for approbation to the Regional Archaeological Service, which can also carry out controls during the whole of the excavation in order to verify the quality. Only upon these verifications does the service give (or not) the authorisation to excavate. Lastly, approval can be withdrawn at any moment in case of serious negligence or fault.

Despite of these precautions, a large proportion of the French archaeological community showed in 2003 its hostility to this measure, through petitions, demonstrations and even strikes. These eight months of crisis were the subject of a special report in the journal *Les Nouvelles de l'archéologie* (no. 95, 2004), of two websites (www.archeo.levillage.org and www.canalarcheo.org) and of an important report on the website of Télévision France 2 (http://cultureetloisir.france2.fr/patrimoine/dossiers/).

The Conseil National de la Recherche Archéologique itself expressed its reservations (*Avis* no. 22, 14th April 2003). It was not only a question of ideological prejudice. Those who were against competition pointed out that in the United States of America and in Britain, as mentioned in the introduction, commercial competition had led to a definite separation between archaeology that we may call 'academic' and private enterprise archaeologists, who publish very little and are hardly ever present at scientific congresses. And even in Britain, where in the Common Law tradition there was hardly any legislation concerning preventive archaeology – apart from a simple circular ('guidance'), the parliamentary report chaired by Colin Renfrew expressed certain reservations (first report of the All-party Parliamentary Archaeology Group, January 2003: it can also be consulted on the websites of English Heritage and the Institute of Field Archaeology).

At present, however, practically no private enterprise has been created in France since 2003, and the only ones present on the market, of very small size, already existed and collaborated with INRAP. Moreover, their prices were not lower than those of INRAP. When no other candidate presents itself, INRAP is given by law the responsibility to carry out the excavation (figure 10.3). And it is also INRAP that, in every case, has to assure the scientific publication of the excavation, after the handing in of the excavation report.

As for the scientific quality control, the system is comparable to that of diagnostic evaluations. For INRAP, the internal control is carried out by the regional scientific assistants of the Scientific Council. For all structures, the external control is carried out by the regional archaeological services of the Ministry of Culture – first for approval, or not, of the excavation project; then during the excavations; and lastly through approval, or not, of the final excavation report. The opinion of the CIRA can also be requested at any moment and visits to some sites by CIRA members are organised regularly.

In this form, the French system, which is certainly not yet fully finalised, expresses well the wish for a strong control by the State considered as representing the community of citizens. It also expresses the idea that the developer is not a simple

Figure 10.3 Excavation of Roman boats found in Lyon (Photo INRAP).

'client' but that he must pay, as a 'polluter' insofar as he impairs national heritage and that he should repair this damage. It also considers that the notion of 'ethical code', very popular in the tradition of the Anglo-Saxon liberal economy, has no meaning in a country of Latin culture where the only valid consideration is written Law.

But the French system also expresses the idea that the scientific conduct of an excavation cannot be compared with the building of a bridge, which is subject to predefined standards and whose quality can be controlled afterwards. As every student learns, an archaeological excavation is first of all an act of destruction: once completed, they can no longer be re-enacted or fully controlled. Moreover, the scientific objectives of an excavation are on each occasion local and context-specific (figure 10.4), unlike the principles governing the building of a bridge. In certain cases and depending on the state of knowledge, if the site belongs to a well known archaeological period, a rapid excavation could be recommended; whereas, in other cases, a much more detailed excavation may be necessary (figure 10.5). There are therefore no pre-established 'standards' which would suffice, as for a bridge, to be controlled afterwards.

Overall, these different points show that in Europe there is a strong divergence as to the role of the State depending on the different cultural traditions.

Figure 10.4 Excavation in the Cour Napoléon at the Louvre museum, Paris (Photo INRAP).

THE EUROPEAN UNION AND THE FUTURE OF PUBLIC SERVICES

A last point, essential for the future of scientific quality control, deals with the evolution of European Law concerning public services in general, and in the domain of preventive archaeology in particular. It is known that the founders of Europe, in a line of action that could be qualified as 'Marxist', or in any case inspired by the Customs Union (*Zollverein*) which facilitated German unification in the 19th century, concentrated the effort for European construction on the creation of a common economic space and a single market. It is in this perspective that, among others, the public services depending on a network (energy, post, transport, and telecommunications) have been little by little privatised and placed in competition

Figure 10.5 Excavation of the wisigothic palace in Toulouse, 5th century AD. (Photo INRAP).

within the framework of 'economic services of general interest'. Another line of action could have been possible, even though the choice has never been presented as such to the European citizens – that of great unified European public services (a European Railway company or a European Postal Service for example). In all cases, these 'network' services also represent important economic issues. But regarding the competitive model, can it be applied indefinitely to the entirety of public services (think of the problems posed by the British railway system and the production and distribution of electricity in the United States)? What would a European society be like, where the whole of the economic, social and cultural activities were uniquely dependent on the market? This question weighed very heavily in the French vote on the project for the EU Constitutional Treaty in 2005.

The European Union has only recently become aware of a shortcoming in this domain, notably by publishing a 'Green Paper on Services of General Interest' (May 21st 2003; English version). This document, enlightening, if not symptomatic, notes that "services of general interest play an increasing role" (par. 2, p. 3) and "are found at the core of the political debate", inasmuch that "public authorities" should "safeguard the general interest, in particular the satisfaction of citizens' essential needs and the preservation of public goods where the market fails" (par. 4, p. 3). However, it also notes that "the term 'services of general interest' cannot be found in the Treaty" of Rome, which only knows the "services of general economic interest" (articles 16 and 86 of the treaty) even though it does not define them (par. 16–17, p. 7). But "it is probably neither desirable nor possible to develop a single comprehensive European definition of the content of services of general interest" (par. 49, p. 15) and "public authorities in each Member State retain considerable freedom to define and enforce public service obligations and to organise the provision of services of general interest" (par. 83, p. 25). In fact, they can be financed through the "State budget" or by "special and exclusive rights (*e.g.* a legal monopoly)" (par. 86, p. 26). Moreover, the evaluation of public services should be "multidisciplinary and multidimensional and include political, economic, social and environmental aspects" (par. 96, p. 29).

To sum up, through this document the Brussels Commission shows its awareness of the limits of regulation by the market (*i.e.* privatisation) of public services. The introduction of competition seems to have had beneficial effects both where the market could exist, and where the quality of service given was directly and easily evaluated (*e.g.* telecommunications). But when one goes beyond these limits, it is obvious, and the Commission recognises this, that the "market" has no reason to reply necessarily to all the aspirations of the citizens of the European Union as regards public services. This is why this Green Paper only aims at opening the debate and finishes (pp. 32–34) with 30 questions to which the "interested parties" are invited to reply electronically, so that the Commission can draw its conclusions and "if necessary, present concrete initiatives as a follow-up" (p. 31). Particularly interesting in terms of the subject treated here are the questions dealing with financing and in particular question 21: "Are you aware of any cases in which the Community law, and in particular the application of State aid rules, has impeded the financing of services of general interest or led to inefficient choices?"; and question 23: "Are there sectors and/or circumstances in which market entry in the form of 'cream-skimming' may be inefficient and contrary to the public interest?" (p. 34).

It is also most interesting that right through this document, the Commission, in spite of an initial effort to distinguish them, hesitates or oscillates constantly between the terms "services of general interest" and "services of general economic interest". Thus, it specifies (par. 96, p. 29) that "in the context of its horizontal evaluation, the Commission has submitted a methodology for the evaluation of services of general interest". But the document to which it refers, in footnote 57, is entitled 'Communication of the Commission: Methodological Note for the Horizontal Evaluation of the Services of General Economic Interest' (COM (2001) 331 Final of 18.06.2002).

The Green Paper ends with an annexe which is longer than the main text itself, and which is entitled 'Public service obligations and instruments of Community policy in the area of services of general economic interest'. The same hesitations are present. In the last part of this annexe, the Commission studies the articulation between the services of general interest and the obligations stemming from the General Agreement on Trade and Services (GATS) on the one hand and the World Trade Organization (WTO) on the other, of which the European Union is an active member. The Commission recalls that "the notion of service of general interest cannot be found in the GATS", but is excluded from GATS "for all sectors, services provided to the public in the exercise of governmental authority, which means any service that is supplied neither on a commercial basis, nor in competition, with one or more service suppliers" (par. 75, p. 64). It states that "The GATS does not require privatisation nor deregulation of services of general interest. It is up to WTO members to decide on these issues in the exercise of sovereign rights. There is no single model of general interest within the WTO membership. The concept varies according to the different sectors and national traditions and legal conditions in the members concerned. The GATS leaves it entirely for members to decide whether they provide services of general interest themselves, directly or indirectly (through public undertakings) or whether they entrust their provision to a third party. Thus, services of general interest can be and are carried out either by public or by private undertakings, or jointly" (par. 78–79, p. 60). Concerning the demands made to the WTO by the European Community for the liberalisation of the service sectors, the Green Paper states that "Through these demands the Community does not seek to dismantle services of general interest nor to privatise state-owned companies in third countries" (par. 88, p. 62).

PROVISIONAL CONCLUSIONS

In conclusion, one can see that the debate is far from being clear-cut. It would be, in this respect, a caricatural vision but sometimes attested, to consider that French legislation, in creating the legal monopoly of INRAP for the evaluations and archaeological excavations (Law of 2001, original version), or at least a monopoly for the diagnostics, shared with the services of the territorial collectives, towns and départements (Law of 2001, amended 2003), should have perpetrated a flagrant violation of the community rules and is against the trend of the general movement of history. In fact, five points should be borne in mind:

1. On April 2nd, 2003 the European Commission rejected the complaints, conducted by the General Department of Competition and directed against the Law of January 17th, 2001 (original). This analysis joins that of the French *Conseil Constitutionnel* (decision of January 16, 2001) but also that of the French *Conseil d'Etat* (decision of April 30, 2003) and even of the French *Conseil National de la Concurrence* (decision of March 13, 2002). The State is thus authorised, if it wishes, to set up a public monopoly of preventive archaeology. From this point of view, the other European countries that already have such a monopoly are authorised to keep it.

2. More generally, having been at the origin of the privatisation of network public services (telecommunications, energy, transport), the European Commission recognises in its Green Paper that the question of services of general interest remains largely to be treated within the European Union and that it is part of the political power to guarantee the general interest "where the market fails".

3. Is preventive archaeology governed by market rules? Or, in other words, is the developer a 'customer' of archaeology? Although it is certain that the developer is obliged by the public power, following the principle of 'polluter pays' ('*casseur = payeur*' in French, or '*Verursacherprinzip*' in German) to pay for the preventive archaeological excavations before each development, is he directly interested in the scientific quality of the excavations and their result? Or is he not simply paying a form of tax, with the state having as it duty to control directly (by carrying out the excavations itself) or indirectly (by a public establishment or other authorised organ) the scientific quality of these excavations and their good exploitation and restoration?

4. Is there an economic reality for such a market of preventive archaeology?

5. When all is said and done, as the Brussels Commission affirms, it is the general interest that is in question. Our general interest orders that our archaeological heritage, according to the Convention of Malta, should be preserved. If it cannot be integrally (conservation of the site *in situ*), then it should be by a quality-controlled preventive excavation. By maintaining the public monopoly of the evaluations, the French government has clearly signified that it wants to guarantee their 'objectivity'. By submitting the possible opening of preventive excavations to private enterprises, the State has nonetheless provided itself with a number of safeguards. Therefore, whatever system is adopted, the quality of the scientific results obtained will be the criterion of the quality of the system.

Thus, as much for France as for Europe, the application of the law, at least in the domain of preventive archaeology, seems to be clearly subordinated to political and cultural choices, if not those of society. For the specialist of the history of human societies, this observation is finally reassuring.

References

All-Party Parliamentary Archaeology Group (2003) *The Current State of Archaeology in the United Kingdom.* London.

Commission of the European Communities (2003) *Green Paper on Services of General Interest* (COM (2003) 270 final). Brussels.

Conseil National de la Recherche Archéologique (2003) *De la concurrence en archéologie*, Avis no.22. (*Les Nouvelles de l'archéologie* 93). Paris.

Demoule, J.-P. (2004) Archéologie préventive, recherche scientifique et concurrence commerciale. In P.-L. Frier (ed.) *Le nouveau droit de l'archéologie préventive*, 199–242. Paris.

Demoule, J.-P. (2002) Rescue Archaeology: the French way. *Public Archaeology* 2, 170–177.

CHAPTER 11

Making it matter: towards a Swedish contract archaeology for social sustainability

Per Lekberg

INTRODUCTION

In our times, a growing number of people in Europe live in places, landscapes, countries, societies where the images of the past, notions of national identity, or indeed the Great Story of the society, have no place for them or their children. We see European societies where the very cement of society, the glue that is supposed to promote solidarity, sense of social duty and interdependence is drying out and cracking up. In these cracks, alternative and for the moment stronger images emerge.

It is high time to accept that contract archaeology is a political act. It depends on national legislation. It is conducted for the benefit of society and its citizens. It produces images of the past at a faster rate and with more resources at hand than any other sector in society involved in producing knowledge of the past. The link that contract archaeology creates again and again between then and now, between soil and citizen has to be taken seriously. Thus, the time has come for a more clear-cut focus on the bigger issues of archaeological knowledge production, on the societal purposes of this knowledge production and on the users of the archaeological knowledge in society.

Any effort to evaluate and ensure quality in contract archaeology has to set out from an assessment of the task of contract archaeology – what society expects contract archaeology to deliver. In this aspect, aims and goals of cultural policy are valid prerequisites along with relevant research objectives, adequate methods and professional reliability in the work of authorities, corporations and commercial companies. Thus, the social settings of Swedish contract archaeology and the Swedish government's aims for heritage policy are presented first in this article. On a general level, quality evaluation in archaeology can never stop short of dealing with how knowledge is produced, what knowledge is produced and how this knowledge is communicated to society. Evaluation of quality in contract archaeology also requires a mapping and delimitation of the process of contract archaeology – its subjects, agents, actions, organisation and economics. Necessary tasks in quality strategies, like balancing cost and quality or balancing power, resources and responsibility, are almost impossible to conduct without a clear cut view of the structures involved, their roles and levels of interdependence. The system of Swedish contract archaeology is currently subjected to reform efforts in a more commercial direction. As suggested by a government appointed commission of inquiry into Swedish contract archaeology, published in a Swedish Government Report (*Statens Offentliga Utredningar*, or SOU, 2005: 80), future contract archaeology should be faced with higher levels of competition in a revised tendering process. In this situation, the National Heritage Board of Sweden seeks to ensure that quality in contract archaeology, and its potential for fulfilling its task in society, is not sacrificed on the altar of market economics. The challenge here is to ensure competition with the objective of quality, since society's purpose for contract archaeology is not primarily to dig cheaply, but to dig meaningfully. Thus, the structures and process of Swedish contract archaeology are discussed in the latter part of the article. Finally, I try to summarise the outlook on quality evaluation in contract archaeology presented in the article.

SOCIETAL SETTINGS FOR CONTRACT ARCHAEOLOGY

Modern, democratic and secular citizen nations require a delicate balance of freedoms and duties, built on a trust in society, on a sense of belonging, founded in images of self, place and past. So, then, the veil between sustainable democracy and conflict-ridden balkanisation is woven with ideas, with images of the past, with trust, with a sense of belonging, with hope for the future. This has to mean something for European contract archaeology in the 21st century.

Swedish contract archaeology is a part of the cultural politics and the heritage policy of Sweden. The governments' political aims and goals for the culture and heritage management thus apply to contract archaeology, even though the actual excavations in growing numbers are carried out by market-based archaeological corporations. Contract archaeology is the quantitatively foremost producer of knowledge of the prehistoric past in Sweden (Kristiansen 1996, 113), and has large economic resources at hand for this work. This bestows on contract archaeologists a high degree of power over the images of the country's past – images conveyed to the Swedish citizens and to people abroad. As power must be balanced with responsibility and transparency in a democratic society, contract archaeology must evolve in response to society's needs and demands for it. Thus, the National Heritage Board of Sweden (*Riksantikvarieämbetet*) is currently working on reformed outlines for contract archaeology.

SOCIETY'S DEMANDS ON CONTRACT ARCHAEOLOGY

Contract archaeology has to fulfil two main, interdependent and integrated roles to succeed in meeting the demands from society. The first role, constituting the very foundation for its existence, is in knowledge production and cultural policy. The prerequisites for succeeding in this role are knowledge production with scientific translucency, and knowledge communication with theoretical awareness and societal responsibility.

Aims for Swedish cultural heritage policy

- A defended and preserved cultural heritage
- A sustainable society with positive and stimulating environments and with the heritage management working as an active force in the reform
- The understanding, involvement and responsibility of all for the cultural environment
- National and international solidarity and respect for the cultural heritage of different groups

Figure 11.1 Aims for Swedish cultural heritage policy.

The second role, wholly dependant on the first, is contract archaeology as a part of society's desired change and restructuring of the physical landscape, for example construction work and infrastructural enterprises. This role demands of contract archaeology a professional and economically reasonable clearance for exploitation, resulting in valuable contributions to archaeological knowledge and cultural policy. Both these roles, and meeting their requirements, are equally important in the quality evaluation of contract archaeology in Sweden.

However, the cultural policy part of contract archaeology's roles has not hitherto been taken into account to an adequate extent. One reason for this might be that the link between material culture, knowledge and images of the past and societal issues, such as social sustainability and identity reproduction (Schama 1995), has been more or less forgotten or taken for granted during the last 30 years or so. In the same time period, changes in society have made it necessary to address such issues and to re-legitimise archaeology as a humanistic, ideographic science capable of relevant statements and valuable contributions to society. Therefore, the National Heritage Board's current work in reforming the outlines for Swedish contract archaeology takes off in an attempt to connect the aims for Swedish cultural policy (figure 11.1) with the objectives of contract archaeology.

A DEFENDED AND PRESERVED CULTURAL HERITAGE

Of course, cultural heritage evolves and it is constantly created, transformed and renegotiated. This is self-evident, sound and positive. Reading the pretexts of Swedish heritage legislation, it becomes clear that defence and preservation of cultural heritage currently mainly refers to the material traces from the past.

Even though contract archaeology recovers most of the retrievable objects when conducting excavations, the concepts of defence and preservation of material cultural heritage might be seen as contradictory to the active destruction of landscape structures connected with contract archaeology. However, good contract archaeology transforms material traces from the past into knowledge, thus aiding the contextualisation, understanding and communication of the cultural heritage. When contextualised, understood and communicated, the physically removed cultural heritage is an aid in the value description, defence and preservation of landscape structures and other material traces from the past. To fulfil this objective, the produced knowledge and communication has to matter to society. Otherwise society will ultimately step back from its preservative legislation and there will no longer be a role for contract archaeology.

A SUSTAINABLE SOCIETY

Archaeology deals with dichotomies, such as now and then, us and them, new and old. The discipline and its history are intimately related to identity matters (Schama 1995) – questions like who am I, where do I come from, who are we, where do we belong? It is intertwined with the history of nationalism and of European nation states. The destructive, often catastrophic consequences, in history as well as in contemporary society, of essentialist nationalism using archaeology for imperialistic or racist ends should be apparent to most Europeans (Smith 2004; Trigger 1993). Nevertheless it has to be emphasised by each generation in order to be avoided. But the constructive, positive connections between archaeology and the growth of democracy in civic nation states has not been stressed to the same extent. Maybe that too, in the same way as the democratic values of European societies, has to be emphasised anew by each generation in order to be applied and not forgotten.

At the birth of industrial society and the demographic revolution in connection with it, archaeology produced and communicated the knowledge and images necessary for sustaining national communities, which in turn provided the platforms for the evolvement of democracy. At least in Sweden, national imagery founded in archaeological knowledge helped develop political democracy and social equality policies, thus further aiding society's sustainability (Magnusson Staaf 2004, 51). In this aspect, archaeology proved a necessary prerequisite for Sweden's evolvement from a socially segregated, deeply religious society into the secular, more socially integrated and democratic nation state of legally equal citizens it is now.

That situation, however, may not be a stable one because growing social and ethnic segregation creates fundamental social sustainability problems for Sweden as well as other European nations. In this situation, archaeology can aid society with perspectives on historical change, identity formation, human universality and individuality through time and space, and perspectives on the use and misuse of material culture. Since legally regulated contract archaeology claims legitimate

Figure 11.2 When the past is bigger than the future, it might stop you from seeing where you are going...

authority in producing knowledge of the past, this knowledge must be produced under demands of scientific translucency. It must be possible to scrutinise the theoretical foundations for knowledge production and its results.

In its communication of knowledge of and perspectives on the past, contract archaeology should emphasize change and cultural integration as the obvious, unavoidable and positive forces in the development process of a culture that they are. The objective for such communication should be to facilitate ethnic and cultural integration, and to encourage solidarity by promoting a widened and renegotiated historical base for the national community. An unreflected emphasis on preservation and reservations might work in the opposite direction.

Archaeology's dealing with the long time spans gives it a perhaps unique potential for boosting public awareness of how culture forms and transforms through history – the constant braiding of continuity and change, of new and old, of foreign and domestic (Kohl 2004; Lundström and Pilvesmaa 1998). Contract archaeology has the possibility to convey these insights about man as a social and cultural being – the human universality that bridges the gaps in time, space and culture – insights that promote the contemporary and the future society as the basis for the nation, rather than golden ages of the past, and that identify our fellow citizens today as our countrymen, rather than the ancestors of old cultures (see Smith 2004) (figure 11.2).

THE UNDERSTANDING, INVOLVEMENT AND RESPONSIBILITY OF ALL

Evaluation of quality in fulfilling the task of contract archaeology demands a definition of what is included in that task. As stated previously, one of contract archaeology's main roles should be communication with the society that it is a part of. This communication of knowledge and images produced by contract archaeology must be developed and diversified. This includes developing interdisciplinary cooperation in matters of communication, but also cooperation between the different parts of the discipline itself, such as universities, regional authorities, museums

Figure 11.3 A cultural landscape in northernmost Sweden.

and excavators. The physically overt potential of relevant excavation sites must be recognised and put to use in this communication.

Material culture is always connected with symbolic meaning, a social sign value (Maquet 1993; Vandkilde 2000). Recognition and naming of material culture are important factors for common participation and responsibility. For instance, landscapes are human constructions, perceivable as multi-purpose arenas for the construction, materialisation and transformation of memory, identity and social order – rooms for social reproduction. This applies to material culture from the past, but also to the formations of landscape (figure 11.3) and the material culture of contemporary society. Material culture is nothing without the cognitive images that give it meaning – shared cultural references to memories, to history (Küchler 1993; Schama 1995; Knapp and Ashmore 1999; Tilley 1993, 81; Bradley 2000, 26; Johnston 1998, 59).

So, communication about identity, culture, history and heritage along the lines mentioned above, the big issues of social sustainability, requires basic communication about what is what and from when, so that some common ground is created. Within the contemporary and social spheres of communication and identification of the material, cultural heritage becomes known, named and understandable. Learning about this together with other people becomes an important tool for the socialisation and orientation of the individual, in the landscape as well as in society (Tilley 1994, 19, 26, 33 and 67; Welinder 1992, 45; Johnston 1998, 62).

Figure 11.4 Young citizens studying material culture from the past together.

This process is comparable with language recognition and learning – material culture as well as language carries with it the ability to express collective meaning (Magnusson Staaf 2000). Knowledge about these things is by no means new. It is connected with the interest in the materiality of social life, and the study of material culture shown by early Enlightenment scholars. For contract archaeologists, this has to be basic pedagogy – teaching and communicating the material language of cultural heritage is a democratic prerequisite. In practise, it starts with systematic cooperation with schools (figure 11.4).

All contract archaeologists, at least those who work under legislative demands of excavation, agree that not all excavations or other archaeological projects stand in the frontline of scientific potential. However, high scientific potential must not be the only recognised potential of an excavation. An excavation may have a high communicative potential, even though the scientific potential is not that thrilling (figure 11.5). For example, a simple fact of geographic proximity to a school might prove important for the communicative potential of the project. So, when relevant, communication should be prioritised over scientific goals of knowledge production as aim for a project. Every euro spent on contract archaeology should matter to society somehow, and the communicative quality of contract archaeology must be emphasised along with the scientific or knowledge-producing aspect of it.

NATIONAL AND INTERNATIONAL SOLIDARITY

As already mentioned above, contract archaeology has a unique possibility, and in fact an obligation to society, to communicate insights that facilitate ethnic and cultural integration. Our identities, individual as well as social and national, are partly formed through the potent mixture of history, social relationships, politics and cultural viewpoints expressed in the landscape around us, in our cultural heritage. In turn, this affects the way we shape and view our contemporary society (Gansum *et al.* 1997; Bender 1993, 3; Donham 1995, 52).

Therefore, contract archaeological communication should encourage civic national solidarity by promoting a widened and renegotiated historical base for the national community. Whatever we choose to say, avoid saying, or refuse to say about the past today has political impact (Donham 1995). It will inevitably colour people's views on their own as well as other peoples identity, on us and them, on contemporary society. Any national community in Europe today, I believe, is obliged to address questions about the nature and contents of its national identity. Essentialism is a strong underflow in European identity ideology (Vermeersch 2004). Too strong not to be scrutinised and challenged by a more fruitful outlook on national identity, as acquirable, renegotiable and citizenship-based (Smith 1986; Ascherson 2003, 58). An unreflected, too strong an emphasis on preservation and reserves in cultural heritage policy may work counterproductively in this respect, creating images of cultural preservation being possible and desirable. In practise, contract archaeology should actively seek communication with people from ethnic minority groups, in order to establish possibilities for dialogue and knowledge integration. Doing this, it is important to avoid falling into the essentialist trap. Only initially in this process the ethnic minority group is identified in order to find people not yet reached by communication. The actual communication takes place with individual citizens, with a right to the cultural heritage of all citizens – the cultural heirs of Sweden.

Figure 11.5 Communicative potential at hand...

Contract archaeology has, as mentioned above, a potential for raising the public awareness of cultural formation and transformation through history. European nations, as indeed all nations and societies, are results of constant braiding of inheriting, lending, borrowing and creolising (Lundström and Pilvesmaa 1998; Källén 2001, 61). In communicating matters of culture and history, contract archaeology has the chance to point out man's likenesses across cultural limits in time and space, as well as man's individuality within these cultural limits. In doing so, contract archaeology promotes international solidarity on the basis of border transgressing human universality, and creates an obligation to actively seek communication with contract archaeology in other countries.

QUALITY CONTROL IN A COMMERCIAL SYSTEM FOR CONTRACT ARCHAEOLOGY

The Swedish system for contract archaeology is based on the Heritage Conservation Act (1988, 950). All ancient monuments and other material culture heritage, whether known or not yet known, is protected by this law. The National Heritage Board supervises the management of heritage resources nationwide, while the County Administrative Board supervises heritage resources in the county. There is a national register listing and describing known ancient monuments, and this register has been kept up to date by revisional surveys carried out by the National Heritage Board. Contractors who are planning to use land containing ancient monuments are obliged to apply to the County Administrative Board for removing the ancient monuments before starting the work. The County Administrative Board may give permission for this, usually demanding that the contactor, in case of going on with his plans, has to pay for an archaeological excavation of the monument. When there are no known monuments in the area of planned construction, the County Administrative Board, or indeed the contractor by his own initiative, can see fit to decide on an archaeological survey with the objective of finding out whether there are ancient monuments there or not. The main principle for decisions is that the County Administrative Board decides who is to carry out the contract archaeology, how much this should cost, and instructs the contractor to make a deal with the chosen archaeological unit. The National Heritage Board may appeal against decisions by the County Administrative Board or by a court of law under the Heritage Conservation Act. When the excavation is over, the archaeological unit reports to the County Administrative Board and to the contractor.

Not long ago, Swedish contract archaeology was subject to a *de facto* monopoly, where the National Heritage Board's own excavation service was the only actor on a national level of larger projects and a formal role-model for quality in contract archaeology. Regional museums acted locally and regionally on a smaller scale, limited to their respective region and expected to adhere to the example of the role model when it came to quality matters. Private archaeological units have had limited success in striving to be assigned work from the County Administrative Board in competition with the Archaeological Excavations Department of the National Heritage Board (*Avdelningen för arkeologiska undersökningar*, UV). The situation that the National Heritage Board is the supervisor of the system where UV is the main actor, and that decisions about UV getting work or not are subjected to the possibility of appeal from the National Heritage Board, has been found more and more dissatisfactory over time.

Partly as a result of this, the system is currently undergoing a shift towards a more commercial, market adjusted practise (SOU 2005: 80 – see above). This situation represents possibilities as well as risks. The aims and goals of Swedish cultural policy stand fast, as do contract archaeology's roles in that cultural policy. The assessment of quality in Swedish contract archaeology is connected with these roles today, and even more in the future. While a commercial system might perhaps lower the costs for contract archaeology, it is far from self-evident that it will prove successful in delivering good quality contract archaeology for that cost. That is, reaching the scientific, communicative and corporate quality requirements that must be connected with Swedish contract archaeology.

With only one team on the field, rules of the game are not so important. Playing the game in full competition is something altogether different. That takes rules, motivation for adherence and systems for control. The referees have to be neutral, able-bodied and competent enough to evaluate the play, so that to ensure the possibility for quality performance. Otherwise, people might get hurt, and the public will lose interest and leave.

To assert the quality of contract archaeology in a commercial system, the National Heritage Board strives to clarify, enhance and strengthen national legislation and regulation regarding heritage management and contract archaeology. Quality has to be defined in order to make evaluation of results and comparison with costs possible. It is preferable that commercial competition focuses on higher quality rather than exclusively on lower costs, and that incentives to help promote this are built into a reformed system. The structure, role-play and process of contract archaeology have to be clarified. The regional authorities, being responsible for the tendering and the outcome of contract archaeology, should control more directly the funding of contract archaeology and monitor more actively its quality and outcome.

IN CONCLUSION

The time has come for a more clear-cut focus on the bigger issues of archaeological knowledge production, on the societal purposes of it and on the users of the archaeological knowledge in society. Knowledge and images of the past must be communicated clearly, with theoretical and political awareness and with responsibility towards society. This, however, does not mean diminished demands of scientific translucency on the methods and results or lesser trust in archaeological method as an acceptable scientific way of producing knowledge of the past. On the contrary, production of knowledge of the past must be subjected to scientific scrutiny in a democratic society, otherwise it is potentially dangerous. For Swedish contract archaeology, this shift of focus is necessary if society at large is to accept its costs in the long run. Quality in contract archaeology, like any other enterprise, can only be assessed and evaluated through comparing objective and outcome. In order to reach an outcome of good quality, Swedish contract archaeology in a future commercial setting has to be subjected to rules of play with more clarity and firmness, and upheld by more active, forceful and knowledgeable authorities on the regional and national levels than before. In such a setting, commercial contract archaeology has the potential for enhancing the quality of the task it is set to perform by and for society. Society has its contract archaeology for a reason. The work it does has to contribute to society to be worth legislation, hassle for constructors and money spent. Contract archaeology has to *matter*.

References

Asherson, N. (2003) Archaeology and nationalism. Special issue of Nations and Nationalism. Margarita Diaz-Andreu. *Public Archaeology* 3, 58–60.

Bender, B. (ed.) (1993) *Landscape: Politics and Perspectives*. Providence/Oxford.

Bolin, H. (ed.) (2004) *The Interplay of Past and Present. Papers from a session held at the 9th annual EAA-meeting in St. Petersburg 2003*. (Södertörn Archaeological Studies 1). Huddinge.

Bradley, R. (2000) *An Archaeology of Natural Places*. London/New York.

Donham, D. L. (1995) *History, Power, Ideology: Central Issues in Marxism and Anthropology. Studies in Marxism and Social Theory*. Paris.

Gansum, T., G. B. Jerpåsen and Ch. Keller (1997) Arkeologisk landskapsanalyse med visuelle metoder. (*AmS-Varia* 28). Stavanger.

Johnston, R. (1998) Approaches to the perception of landscape. Philosophy, theory, methodology. *Archaeological Dialogues* 5, 54–68.

Knapp, A. B. and W. Ashmore (1999) Archaeological Landscapes: Constructed, Conceptualized, Ideational. In W. Ashmore and A. B. Knapp (eds.) *Archaeologies of landscape: contemporary perspectives*, 1–32. Malden.

Kohl, P. L. (2004) Comments on Adam T. Smith´s 'The end of the essential archaeological subject'. *Archaeological dialogues* 11, 20–21.

Kristiansen, K. (1996) Old Boundaries and New Frontiers. Reflections on the Identity of Archaeology. *Current Swedish Archaeology* 4, 103–122.

Küchler, S. (1993) Landscape as Memory: The Mapping of Process and its Representation in a Melanesian Society. In B. Bender (ed.) *Landscape: Politics and Perspectives*, 85–106. Oxford.

Källén, A. (2001) Creolised Swedish Archaeology. *Current Swedish Archaeology* 9, 59–76.

Lundström, I. and M. -L. Pilvesmaa (1998) Reflections on an Unreflected Sphere. Archaeological Exhibitions and Nationalism. *Current Swedish Archaeology* 6, 143–151.

Magnusson Staaf, B. (2000) Form and Function – the Architecture of Meaning. In D. Olausson and H. Vandkilde (eds.) *Form, Function & Context. Material Culture Studies in Scandinavian Archaeology*, 71–80. (Acta Archaeologica Lundensia Series 8: 31). Lund.

Magnusson Staaf, B. (2004) To Remodel Society – Democracy and Archaeology. In H. Bolin (ed.) *The Interplay of Past and Present. Papers from a session held at the 9th annual EAA meeting in St. Petersburg 2003*, 51–56. (Södertörn Archaeological Studies 1). Huddinge.

Maquet, J. (1993) Objects as Instruments, Objects as Signs. In S. Lubar and W. D. Kingery (eds.) *History from Things. Essays on Material Culture*, 30–40. Washington/London.

Schama, S. (1995) *Landscape and Memory*. London.

Smith, A. D. (1986) *The Ethnic Origins of Nations*. Oxford.

Smith, A. T. (2004) We, they, and I. Politics after the end of essential archaeological subjects. *Archaeological dialogues* 11, 27–36.

Tilley, C. (1993) Art, Architecture, Landscape (Neolithic Sweden). In B. Bender (ed.) *Landscape: Politics and Perspectives*, 49–84. Oxford.

Tilley, C. (1994) *A Phenomenology of Landscape: Places, Paths and Monuments.* Oxford/Providence.

Trigger, B. G. (1989) *A History of Archaeological Thought.* New York.

Vandkilde, H. (2000) Material Culture and Scandinavian Archaeology: A Review of the Concepts of Form, Function and Context. In D. Olausson and H. Vandkilde (eds.) *Form, Function & Context. Material culture studies in Scandinavian archaeology,* 3–49. (Acta Archaeologica Lundensia Series 8: 31). Lund.

Vermeersch, P. (2004) Archaeology and identity politics. A cross-disciplinary perspective. *Archaeological dialogues* 11, 22–26.

Welinder, S. (1992) *Människor och landskap.* Aun 15. Uppsala.